Accelerated DevOps with AI, ML & RPA

Non-Programmer's Guide to AIOPS & MLOPS

STEPHEN FLEMING

Accelerated DevOps with AI, ML & RPA

Copyright © 2019 Stephen Fleming

DEDICATION

I DEDICATE THIS BOOK TO THE INNER VOICE
IN ALL OF US, WHICH SOMEHOW ALWAYS
SHOWS US THE RIGHT PATH, IF WE ARE PAYING
ATTENTION.

BONUS TECHNOLOGY BOOKLET

Dear Friend,

I am privileged to have you onboard. You have shown faith in me and I would like to reciprocate it by offering the maximum value with an amazing booklet which contains the latest technology updates.

"Get Instant Access to Free Booklet and Future Updates"

- Link: http://eepurl.com/dge23r

OR

- QR Code: You can download a QR code reader app on your mobile and open the link:

My other Books:

- DevOps Handbook
- Microservices Architecture Handbook
- DevOps and Microservices
- Kubernetes Handbook
- SRE Handbook
- The DevOps Engineer's Career Guide

Table of Contents

1. Introduction to accelerated DevOps

Technological advances such *as predictive analytics, auto computing (autonomics), artificial intelligence, and robotic process automation (RPA)* are currently motivating exceptional levels of automation in many other organizations. Put together; these three technological innovations are driving the next generation of automation-- what is regularly referred to as *"intelligent or smart automation."* Smart automation goes more than simple automation and orchestration of human tasks to integrate flexible self-learning-- leading to entirely autonomous systems. The Google car (and other similar solutions) is an excellent example of an intelligent automatic system capable of knowing from its environment and modifying attributes as necessary.

Automation in Classical DevOps

The electronic process is motivated through new-age modern technologies such as *social, mobile, big data, analytics, cloud, internet of things (IoT), artificial intelligence, augmented and virtual reality, genomics,* etc.

These solutions bring up considerable change and complexity to how modern systems are created and released. Enterprises that leverage these technologies to improve themselves into *intellectual enterprises* ask for fresh and smart methods. Such techniques and procedures need to be more than agile; they need to adaptive and capable of responding dynamically to frequently changing conditions.

Let's look at some samples of recent DevOps approaches and how they will need to evolve to support dynamic digital systems.

Automation within regular DevOps solutions is usually restricted to *scripting and orchestration.* Automation acceptance levels vary due to various reasons ranging from intricacy to skills and organizational challenges. Upkeep of such scripts is itself sometimes a bottleneck, as applications and environments change rapidly, new age agile, a digital company, by contrast, demand automation that is in a position to adapt dynamically and self-heal on the requirement.

Further, classic DevOps automation procedures are normally driven with predefined static rules. For example, the criteria for the promotion of an application build through various stages of the pipeline are often statically described. This is a restriction for new-age solutions where the *criteria need to be dynamic* and may vary based on multiple situations. The automation solution needs to able to look at past data, keep learning from recent data, and make flexible, intelligent forecasts about the right course of action.

DevOps for the (IoT) process is different than that for conventional software solutions. The intended environment for production deployment in consumer IoT is geographically scattered, typically not configuration managed, may have an undependable network connection, and may even be fragile. Further, IoT solutions generate huge amounts of data that demand robust data mining and self-learning (flexible) techniques not provided through traditional lifecycle automation tools.

Similarly, **customer experience (CX)** is a key new metric for online digital systems that transcends regular DevOps metrics, including release velocity and quality. CX data is disorganized, fuzzy, voluminous, and volatile. CX-driven DevOps (or CX-Ops) is an emerging discipline that requires big data analytics and intellectual strategies (including natural language processing or NLP) to decode meaningful insight from such data.

Hence, as digital enterprises develop and businesses demand greater agility and flexibility, the DevOps function to support such a process will need to change as well.

Intelligent DevOps: Era of Smart Automation Landscape

Right before we dive into what *intelligent DevOps* would look like, let's first look and feel at the several types of automatic systems being adapted in the marketplace in general. The following types of automation are defined as part of the "intelligent automation procession":

Solution that Does: These kinds of are standard automatic systems that replicate human keystroke actions and fixed (pre-defined) rules-based activities. They also take benefit of descriptive analytics that shows past fads and trends. Instances of such systems consist of speech and image recognition.

Solution that Think: These use formulas and knowledge to find the definition in data, manage judgment-oriented tasks using diagnostic analytics, and make referrals based on trends. Examples of such systems consist of natural language processing and recommendation engines (such as email spam filters).

Solution that Learn: These kinds of understand the context, translate and dynamically adjust based on scenarios; they normally take advantage of predictive and prescriptive analytics to solve problems separately. Examples of such systems include self-driving vehicles and neural networks.

A Peek at Intelligent DevOps

So, what would transformed smart DevOps look like? Smart DevOps automatic would take benefit of *cognitive and autonomics systems* to enable smarter adaptive lifecycle automatic based on analytics. Smart DevOps, to a substantial degree, relies on this kind of capability.

Based on the above model, let's check the variety of DevOps automatic we can work upon:

DevOps Solutions that Do: This includes *traditional DevOps automated systems* (e.g., for constant integration and testing, continuous deployment), as well as pipeline lifecycle automated that are based on static rules (e.g., traditional release management automatic).

DevOps Solutions that Think: This consists of advanced automation systems such as:

- Automated automation systems, for instance, generation of automated test cases from manual tests (or test models) using NLP, generation of virtual services based on request-response information logs.

- Self-healing automatic, for instance, virtual services (or test scripts) that can auto-update based on a change in application endpoints (or behavior).

- Surveillance of IoT systems, for example, *"smart homes,"* which require continuous use of diagnostic analytics to mine massive quantities of data to understand failing modes and recommend recovery techniques.

11

- Automated verification of system demands based on customer experience analytics.

- Self-production of test scenarios based on analytics on development logs.

DevOps Systems that Learn: This consists of sophisticated test automation systems such as:

- Flexible continuous delivery pipeline-- Discovering systems that analyze past data to manage the pipeline based on dynamic rules. For example, associate code top quality and flaw detection and slippage patterns to dynamically determine that which tests are to be run and which gates are to be enforced for various teams and products for promoting application builds

- DevOps procedure optimization based on insight throughout the life cycle. For example, the relationships of production log data with past code change data to determine the level of failure risk in different application components.

Cross-Life Cycle DevOps Intellect

Smart DevOps enables us to perform procedure optimization based on analytics from data correlated across the system life cycle, from planning through an operation. Each procedure area generates a great amount of data that is normally evaluated within the process (and sometimes organizational) silo.

While such analytics is useful in itself, the connection of data throughout these procedure areas may be used to provide a wide variety of intelligent lifecycle insight (and procedure improvement possibilities), such as:

- Correlating configuration data analytics with code change and flaw analytics helps us proactively recognize failing modes related to code and infrastructure changes.
- CX analytics (from the Operations procedure) can be used to validate requirements in the plan and define procedures
- Production log analytics may be associated to test log data to identify missing out on test cases. As per the "Continuous Delivery" concept in DevOps, we visualize a new option stream around "Continuous Insight" where analytical understandings are generated and acted upon continuously (and autonomously) as procedures carry out.

So, we believe that intelligent approaches described above will be infused into every aspect of DevOps going onward and reinvent the way DevOps is performed.

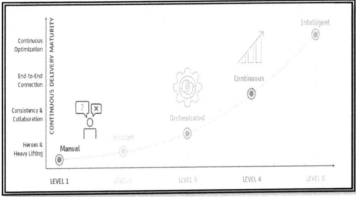

Diagram from Devops.com

The new DevOps with AI & ML

Modern technology advancements have taken the

production abilities of firms to various limits practically across every market.

Long gone are the days where we use to see only human-intensive jobs!

Now, the world is high on technology-driven systems that eased industry processes, from developing a product to releasing it to the market and further towards offering a memorable experience to end-users.

DevOps is one technology service most heard in today's tech world, especially for boosted collaboration among teams and offering faster execution with less failure & high recovery rate.

In the IT industry, DevOps showed up as a solution for abilities such as continuous integration, continuous delivery, and accelerated development rate, among others, that can fasten the software process chain. That's not an end!

There are two of today's most advanced innovations that every other innovation or market would want to scale-up their performance and productivity. While some of the leading market players are already running on them, there are many medium and small-sized still on the run for them. They are undoubtedly ***Artificial Intelligence (AI) and Machine Learning (ML)!***

Applying static tools for *deployments, provisioning, and Application Performance Monitoring (APM)* has currently seen its full potential and is getting soaked up by the ever-growing industry demands.

And, the next mission has already begun *for creative managing tools that can apply knowledge simplifying the task of development and testing engineers.* Here is where Ai and ML play vital roles!

We will see how AI and ML integrations can power DevOps. In brief, AI and ML help DevOps by automating routine & repeatable tasks; offering enhanced effectiveness, and minimizing teams' time spent on a procedure. Let's look into more details!

Basic Concepts: Cut the Clutter

*Artificial Intelligence is the wider principle of equipments being able to carry out jobs in a method that we would take into consideration "smart".

*Machine Learning is a current application of AI based around the idea that we need to actually simply be able to provide machines access to data as well as let them find out on their own.

AI in DevOps

A data revolution is one key aspect that is posing severe challenges to the DevOps atmosphere.

Checking through vast quantities of information to find an important issue as part of day-to-day computing operations is time-consuming and human-intensive.

That's where AI has its role in processing, evaluating, and making an instant decision that a human might take hours together to decide on.

With the evolution of DevOps, two different teams started collaborating on a single platform, which needs reliable tools that can reduce the event of errors and revisits a problem.

AI can transform the DevOps setting in various ways, such as:

- *Data Ease of access:* AI can increase the scope of data accessibility to the teams who typically face issues such as lack of freely-available data. AI improves the teams' ability to obtain accessibility to vast quantities of online data beyond business limits for big data gathering. It helps organizations to have well-organized information checked from widely-available datasets for *constant and repetitive evaluation.*

- *Self-governed Solutions:* Adjustment to change is one essential limiting that many firms have been facing owing to a lack of appropriate analytics that restrict themselves to certain borders. Whereas, AI has transformed the scenario bringing in a transition in analysis from being human to self-governed. Now, self-governed tools can drive many procedures that human beings might not be able to that quickly.

- *Resource Management:* Improving range for the production of automated atmospheres that run automate many routine and repeatable jobs, AI transformed the process of resource administration opening more methods for development and creating new techniques.

- *Software Development:* AI's capability to automate many of the service plans and support information analytics is common to have a more critical effect on DevOps atmosphere. Many firms have already begun taking on AI and Machine Learning for achieving effectiveness in application growth.

AI can help your groups in precisely determining the solution to your problem from a dataset rather than spending hours with each other on huge data volumes.

It not only saves time but also reduces the quantity of work.

Machine Learning (ML) impact on DevOps

ML System's too automated learning abilities speak the effective implementation of ML capabilities, which means making it culture the *'practice of continuous learning.'*

It is simpler for the team to deal with complex aspects such as linear styles, datasets, and query refining, and identifying new insights continuously at the speed of their executing platform.

Being part of the procedure chain, ML helps in easy repairing of code in case of bugs and streamlines the process.

Below areas defines the integration of ML and DevOps:

- *Application Progress*: While DevOps tools such as 'Git,' Ansible, among others provide the visibility of delivery procedure, applying ML to them addresses the irregularities around code quantities, long construct time, delays in code check-ins, slow launch rate, improper resourcing, and procedure slowdown, among others.

- *Quality Check*: With a detailed evaluation of testing outputs, ML performs efficient testimonial Quality Assessment results and builds test pattern libraries based on discovery. This keeps alive the thorough testing in case of every launch, thus improving the quality of applications delivered.

- *Protecting Application Distribution*: Safeguarding application shipment is one essential benefit that ML integration offers to DevOps. With ML in place, it's easy to recognize user habits.

- *Dealing with Production Cycles*: DevOps groups generally use ML for analyzing utilization of resource. ML's benefit of possessing a better understanding of application or production makes it apt in managing production issues.
- Addressing Emergencies: Here is the crucial role of ML due to its ability to analyze machine intelligence. ML leads well with the production chain, especially in dealing with sudden alerts by training systems continuously on identifying repeating trends and inadequate warnings, thus filtering the process of immediate signals.

- *Triage Analytics*: ML tools can help you recognize issues in general processing and also manage release logs to create coordination with new deployments.
- *Early Discovery*: ML tools provide Ops teams the ability to detect an issue at an early stage and ensure faster response times, allowing company continuity.

- *Company Assessment*: Not just supporting the procedure advancement, ML also ensures business continuity of the organization. While DevOps performs well in terms of accomplishing service goals, ML tools deal that with its pattern-based functionality by examining user metrics and alert the worried service teams and coders in case of any problem.

Below are the ways in which ML helps DevOps:
- *IT Operations Analytics (ITOA).*
- *Predictive Analytics (PA).*
- *Artificial Intelligence (AI).*
- *Algorithmic IT Operations (AIOps).*

Here are points that should be looked into for AI/ML driven DevOps:

- *Adaptation of APIs*: Moving development teams to gain hands-on experience in working with canned APIs like Azure, AWS, and GCP that allow the deployment of robust AI/ML capacities into their application without having to make models. They can later try on integrating add-ons such as voice-to-text and other innovative designs.

- *Identifying Related Models*: The next action after the above would be identifying similar AI/ML APIs.

- *Parallel Pipeline:* Provided the fact that AI and ML are at the trial and error stage, parallel pipelines remove the vulnerability of the system in case of failure and generates redundancy.

- *Pre-trained Model*: A well-documented, pre-trained model can considerably cut down the threshold for the adoption of ML and AI capacities.

- *Public Data*: The initial data set finding is a crucial

challenge in adopting AI/ML. None would actually feed this information. So, where will you drive information from? That's where you require public data sets. It may not exactly meet your full requirements but can at least fill the spaces to improve project practicality.

- *Due Identification:* The successful implementation has to be shared as case studies for adaptation.

Techniques AI and ML Will Change DevOps for the Better

There's been a lot of media attention in recent years about how artificial intelligence (AI) and machine understanding (ML) are going to change the world-- how they're going to develop new and interesting applications in fields as diverse as education and learning, law, health care, and transportation.

This may happen. If we have to consider a use case where AI and ML will develop a concrete, lasting impact, we are putting the chips on DevOps. DevOps is all about the automation of tasks. Its focus is on automating and checking every step of the software distribution process, ensuring that work gets done swiftly and frequently.

AI and ML are very well suited for DevOps process. They can process vast quantities of details, and help perform menial tasks, freeing the IT staff to do more targeted work. They can learn patterns, anticipate problems, and recommend options. If DevOps' goal is to *unify advancement and operations, AI and ML can smooth out some of the tensions that have separated the two disciplines in the past.*

Here are ways AI and ML can and will change DevOps for the better.

Promoting Comments on Efficiency

One of the properties of DevOps is the use of continuous feedback loops at every stage of the process. This includes using monitoring tools to provide responses to the functional efficiency of running applications. This is one area today where ML is impacting DevOps already. *Monitoring platforms gather huge quantities of data in the form of performance metrics, log files, and other types.* Advanced keeping track of platforms is applying machine learning to these datasets to recognize problems very early and make referrals proactively. These recommendations go to the DevOps team members so that they can ensure that the application service remains viable. Machine discovering is enhancing the continuous comments loops that are essential to DevOps.

Enabling Communication

Communication and responses are always one of the biggest challenges when organizations relocate to a DevOps method. Human interaction is vital, but with so much information moving through the system, teams need to set up a wider range of channels to set and revise workflows on the fly. Using automation technology, chat bots, and other systems initiated by AI, these interactions channels can become more streamlined and more aggressive.

Correlate Data across Platforms and Tools

To operate efficiently, DevOps teams need to streamline tasks. This is getting more challenging as settings get more complex. Start with monitoring tools: Teams tend to use several tools that keep an eye on an application's health and efficiency in different ways. Machine learning applications can soak up these data streams and find relationships, giving the team a more alternative view of the application's total health.

Manage a Flurry of Alerts

Since DevOps motivates teams *to "fail but fail fast,"* it's critical to have an alert system that spots a flaw rapidly. This tends to develop situations where informs are coming fast and furious, all labeled with the same extent, making it challenging for teams to react. Machine understanding applications can help teams prioritize their responses based on factors such as past behavior, the magnitude of the current alert, and the source that certain messages are coming from. We can set up rules, but machines can help manage situations when too much data bewilders the system.

Examining Past Performance

AI/ML also has the prospective to help developers during the application production process. By examining the success of past applications in terms of build/compile success, effective testing conclusion, and functional efficiency, machine understanding algorithms could make recommendations to developers proactively based on the code they are publishing or the application that they are creating. The AI engine could direct the developer on how to construct the most reliable and highest-quality application.

Software Testing

In the future, we could see AI/ML applied to other stages of the software development life cycle to provide enhancements to a DevOps approach or approach. One location where this may happen could be in the area of software testing. Unit tests, regression examinations, functional examinations, and user acceptance tests all create large quantities of data in the form of test results. This info could then notify the advancement teams so that they can come to be more efficient in the future.

DevOps with Cloud and AI: Trinity of Automation

Do you think it is possible to set up an entire IT infra without having known anything - most likely with few lines of common message; and run IT procedure without having understanding much about it - by utilizing simple chat or voice directions? The answer is YES and is topic to imagination & technical constraints.

The answer is a mix of Cloud, DevOps, and Artificial Intelligence (AI).

The need for intelligent ways for IT infrastructure

'IT Infra & Operation' is enduring a major revamp in the modern these days due to infusion of technologies such as cloud computing, automation, machine learning, IoT, and containerization. With growing work, enhanced the pace of development, exponential data development, and users in the its challenging for the conventional setup to match the agility of the new system. At the same time, we can not afford to have a multiyear system implementation. Hence, it is imperative to infuse software knowledge for making an agile, modular architecture which takes the best of Cloud, DevOps and AI.

Let's now understand the fundamental shape of these to venture into brand-new fascination:

Cloud-- Adoption of Cloud-First is currently in place. Cloud technology has been instrumental in every aspect of IT infra-- solution, delivery, and procedures.

DevOps - It is obvious that DevOps is advancing swiftly, though the direction and destination of development are still open to guesses. DevOps is meant for streamlining and automating all aspects of software delivery procedure, specifically in automating infrastructure - Infra as a Code (IaaC).

'DevOps & Cloud' has currently become an appealing mix for many companies across the world. Though cloud and DevOps are various recommendations, they are intertwined, and this combination provides agility and efficiency in IT operations. Automated IT infrastructure is currently well-known.

The containerization with the help of orchestration tolls like Kubernetes, Docker swarm, etc has *automated the deployment model for entire cloud infra* and provided much needed agility.

AI will also expand the boundaries of IT framework automation. Future will see smart infra powered by sophisticated algorithms utilizing ML, NLP, and Deep Learning resulting into smart CI/CD pipeline.

Ideal combinations would be to have an AI-OPS tool that proactively detects the cloud infra need and ideally manages the demand making use of automated DevOps pipeline. The entire procedure will consist of applying ML models to do the historical data analysis and forecast the future of operations on a timeline, highlighting the prospective concerns and recommending possible removal. We are at the cusp of the changes which would be brought by the trinity of DevOps, Cloud and AI. The standard process shall consist of embedded intelligence to automate applications/infra, self-learning applications, and self and inbuilt governance powered by analytics.

Use cases in IT infra

- *Unsupervised machine learning* on substantial data (produced by disparate systems) - Generate correlation of events, acknowledge styles and discover anomalies

- *Forecast or predictions*-- Determine when a metric will hit the threshold, perform 'what if' scenarios, and take preventive activities before a failing happens

- *The root cause analysis*-- Continuously associate data points and pinpoint to a feasible problem and its removal

- *Cost optimization* (use situation of cloud migration)-- Given various input parameters and known output of lowest cost, a monitored ML model to generate cost-optimized cloud migration plan can be constructed in all possibilities

- *Noise reduction* - Lessen noise from the group of alerts, events, logs and simplify the workflows using ML models

- *AI-based DevOps analytics* - Produce the functional metrics to accurately determine the success of DevOps implementation (AI in DevOps).

- *DevOps concept of iterations* - Accelerate the process to train the AI algorithm on the ever-changing AI Versions (DevOps in AI).

- *NLP based ChatOps* - Develop a new setting, spin around up a new resource in the Cloud, or create on-demand infra utilization metrics (AI in Cloud infra).

Symbiotic adoption of AI, Cloud, and DevOps

Deep learning and machine learning are now gradually becoming mainstream. We no longer need to recognize the mathematical jargon like 'stochastic gradient descent' or 'back propagation' to use deep learning ideas. We will also not have to compose a thousand lines of python code to construct a native Chabot. Hundreds of machine learning/deep learning designs are now offered as managed service on the Cloud, with lots of AI tools provided by the cloud service providers.

Cloud service providers are making it easy to run the ML on their platform. They are offering virtual machines (VM) based on the graphics processing unit (GPU) to develop ML applications in the Cloud, APIs for pre-build designs, and natural language processing (NLP) engines to combine with the applications. Organizations are making AI more accessible to individual developers. AWS PageMaker is one such initiative to create a machine learning kit available to familiar designers for building intelligent applications. The products/services built-in with machine learning algorithms, like sentiment analysis, predictive algorithms, and deep learning versions.

So, the mix of AI, DevOps, and Cloud are likely going to change the way business is carried out across domains. DevOps and AI will keep becoming prominent in the value chain of modern technology combined with Cloud. Smart automation will become the new normal, driving innovations and standards. Enterprises should start locating ways to ingest implied knowledge into their IT ecosystem. We all need to be prepared to accept this new technology wave for survival.

Let's see whether this trinity (AI +DevOps+ Cloud) can anticipate, behave, deal with, and take care of companies better than humans in the future.

DevOps with Emerging Technologies like Cloud, IoT, Blockchain, AI/ML, Containers, and DevOps

Many emerging technologies impacting the Enterprise IT ecosystem has come in the same time frame. Let us analyze these technologies and their impact on the service industry.

Also, check the relationship between these technologies. Certainly, each development can and does have a certain value by them. However, when grouped, they can provide powerful services to help drive growth and new business models.

- *Hybrid Cloud, IoT, and AI/ML.* The data produced by application of these technologies causes two primary outcomes: a) immediate verification to find out IoT endpoint or b) accumulate and look for patterns analysis. Both ways, the public cloud is going to offer the most economical service for IoT.

- *IoT & Blockchain.* Blockchains is a distributed ledger which stores data and when works in tandem with machine driven entries we can have non refutable proof of transactions. This is a better way to keep track of the chain of custody, not just law enforcement but subject to spoiling, such as meat and plants.

- *Containers, DevOps, and agile software development.* These form the basis for providing solutions like those above quickly and economically, bringing allowing the value to be realized rapidly by the organization.

There are companies that are already using these technologies to supply innovative solutions. These stories show strong forward momentum; they also tend to foster a belief that these innovations have reached an adequate level of maturity, such that the service is not prone to lack of availability. This is far from the case. Indeed, these innovations are far from mainstream.

Let's discover what fostering means to IT and the business for these various technologies.

Hybrid Cloud

The reason we chose a hybrid cloud versus a public cloud because it stands for an even better amount of complexity to enterprise IT than the public cloud alone. It requires cooperation and integration between organizations and departments that have a common goal but very different methods of achieving success.

First, the cloud is about handling and delivering software services, whereas the data center is charged with providing infra and application. But, the complicated and overhead of managing and supplying reputable and available infrastructure outweigh the complexity of software services, causing the latter often receiving far less attention in most self-managed environments. When the complexity bordering the delivery of infrastructure is gotten rid of, the operations team can focus entirely on the delivery and usage of application.

As we understand that the Security perspective is always a concern, but the maturation process surrounding the delivery of cloud-based applications by the top CSPs confirms that the ecosystem is ever changing. With a Security solution on Cloud the applications are safe.

It demands that after each update to the security controls around. The core team consisting of architects, .coders, operations must analyze the implications of the change and how it would impact the overall application. Any miscalculation of these changes could cause overall system at risk.

A hybrid cloud also often means that the team must retain traditional data center skills while also adding abilities associated with the CSPs (cloud service providers).

It may be most of the times overlooked while assessing cloud costs. Also, highly-skilled cloud personnel are still difficult to attract and generally require high pay package. It is better if you up skill your own staff, but you will want a few specialists in the team on-the-job training for the public cloud because unsecured public cloud may lead to compromising situations for the organization.

Internet-of-Things (IoT).

The concern with IoT is that it is not one single thing, but a complicated network of physical and mechanical parts. In an environment that has been moving to a high degree of virtualization, IoT stands for a shift back toward data center skills with a focus on device configurations, separated states, limitations on the size of data packages being traded, and low-memory code footprint

As everything, digital security is a highly complicated topic concerning IoT. There are so many levels within an IoT solution that invites compromise: the sensor, the network, the edge, the endpoint and much more. For several, nonetheless, when you state IoT, they right away only see the logical aspects related to all the data collected from the myriad of gadgets. Sure, evaluating the data acquired from the sensor mesh and also the edge gadgets can produce an understanding of the means things functioned in methods that were very hard with the coarse-grained telemetry provided by these gadgets. For instance, a production gadget that signaled issues with a low hum prior to the use of sensors that now disclose that in tandem with the hum, there's likewise a rise in temperature level as well as a boost in resonance. With a few short months of accumulating information, there's no demand to also wait on the hum; the information will suggest the beginning of an issue.

Of training course, the worth discussed in the previous paragraph can just be shared if you have the appropriate competent individuals throughout the whole information chain. Those able to customize or set up endpoint devices to take part in an IoT scenario, the cyber security as well as infosec experts to restrict possible issues because of breach or misuse, and also the data scientists with the ability to make feeling of the quantities of information being gathered. Obviously, if you haven't selected the public cloud as the endpoint for your data, you likewise, after that have the extra overhead of taking care of network connectivity and storage space ability monitoring connected with rapidly growing quantities of data.

Artificial Intelligence and also Machine Learning (AI/ML).

If you can harness the power of artificial intelligence and also AI you acquire insights into your service and industry in such a way that was extremely difficult up till recently. While this is seemingly a basic statement, the word "harness" is loaded with complexity. Initially, these technologies are most effective when running versus substantial amounts of information.

The even more data you have, the even more exact the results. This indicates that it is incumbent upon the organization to a) find, aggregate, clean and also keep the data to support the initiative, b) develop a hypothesis, c) assess the outcome of numerous formulas to determine which will best support the result you are looking for-- e.g. anticipating, patterns, and so on-- and also d) create a version. This requires lot of manpower and efforts to get the work done. As soon as your design is full and also your hypothesis is shown, the equipment will certainly do the majority of the work from there on out however, obtaining there requires a great deal of human knowledge engineering initiative.

A word of caution, make company decisions making use of the result of your AI/ML versions when you have actually not complied with every one of these steps .

Blockchain

Promoted as the technology that will certainly "alter the globe," yet outside of cryptocurrencies, blockchain is still attempting to develop firm origins within the service world. There are lots of issues with blockchain adoption at the minute; one of the most common ones is the velocity of modification. There is no solitary typical blockchain innovation.

There are numerous modern technologies, each trying to give the foundation for trusted as well as verified transactional exchange without requiring a centralized party. Buying right into a specific modern technology at this moment in the maturation contour, will offer insight right into the worth of blockchain, however, will certainly call for continuous care and feeding as well as the potential need to move to an entirely various network structure at some time in the future. Thus, don't bet the farm on the strategy you select today.

Furthermore, there are still numerous impressive non-technical concerns that blockchain value is reliant upon, such as the validity of blockchain access as a type of nondeniable. So, can we use blockchain as a legal proof to show intent and recognition of concurred upon activities? There are also concerns connected to what effect usage of a blockchain may carry various partnering agreements as well as debt agreements, especially for worldwide firms with GDPR requirements.

Ultimately, is the value of the blockchain a big enough network to implement consensus? Who should host these nodes? Are the public systems sufficient for a company or exists a need for a private network shared amongst a community with everyday demands?

Containers, DevOps, & Agile SDLC

I have actually abided these three advancements with each other due to the fact that unlike the others, they are extra technical in nature and carry elements of the "just how" extra so than the "what." Still, there is a considerable amount of interest being paid to these three topics that expand much outside the IT organization due to their organization with allowing services to come to be much more dexterous. To wit, I add my general, please note and word of caution, the technology is just an enabler, it's what you make with it that may be useful or may have a contrary impact.

Containers must be the least impactful of these three topics, as it's just another method to make use of computing resources. Containers are smaller sized as well as more light-weight than virtual makers; however, they make sure to isolate instances running inside and outside the container and also what is running outside the container. The intricacy arises from relocating processes from bare metal as well as virtual makers into containers as containers utilize equipment sources in different ways than the abovementioned systems.

While it's rather easy to develop a container, getting a team of containers to interact reliably can be laden with difficulties. This is why container management systems have become a growing number of intricate in time. With the addition of Kubernetes, services properly need the knowledge of data facility operations in a single team. Obviously, public cloud providers now provide taken care of container monitoring systems that decrease the demands on such a broad set of understanding, yet it's still incumbent on operations to know just how to set up and also arrange containers from a performance and also safety and security viewpoint.

DevOps, as well as the Agile Software Advancement Lifecycle (SDLC), actually compel the internal design groups to assume and also act in different ways if they are transitioning from conventional waterfall advancement techniques. Several businesses have taken the primary step of this change by starting to take on some Dexterous SDLC techniques. However, due to the requirement for retraining, hiring, as well as the support of this effort, the interim state most of these companies remain in have actually been called *"wagile,"* indicating some mix of falls as well as Agile.

When it comes to DevOps, the metrics have actually been released pertaining to the business value of ending up being a high-performing software shipment and procedures company. In this age of "software is consuming the globe," can your organization ignore DevOps and otherwise ignore, take years to change? You will certainly hear stories from services that have actually adopted DevOps as well as Agile SDLC as well as made terrific strides in minimizing latency, raising the variety of releases they can make in provided time duration, as well as deploying brand-new abilities and features to production at a much faster rate with less change failures. Many of these stories are actual, but even in these services, you will certainly still find pockets where there is no fostering, and they still adhere to a waterfall SDLC that takes ten months to obtain a solitary launch into manufacturing.

To conclude the Chapter...

Independently, each of these advancements calls for trained resources, financing, and it can be hard to relocate beyond proof-of-concept to completely operationalised manufacturing results.

Absorbed combination, on top of existing operational pressures, these developments can quickly overwhelm even one of the most adept enterprise IT organizations. Also, in cases where it is multi-modal IT and these developments are occurring outside the path of traditional IT, existing IT understanding and also experience will certainly be required to support. For instance, if you intend to evaluate buying patterns for the past five years, you will certainly need to assistance of the teams liable for your monetary systems.

All this brings about a really huge concern, how should organizations set about absorbing these developments?

The pragmatic solution is, of course, present those innovations connected to a specific business outcome. Nonetheless, as specified, waiting to introduce a few of these innovations can cause losing ground to the competition.

This implies that you may desire to present some proof-of-concept projects, *especially around AI/ML, as well as Dexterous SDLC with IoT as well as Blockchain projects* where they make good sense for your business.

So, let's go ahead and understand the AIOPS and MLOPS and what will they do exactly to make our lives easier.

Basic Concepts: Cut the Clutter

AIOPS as per Gartner: According to Gartner, AIOps is defined as the application of machine learning and data science to IT operations problems.

*MLOPS as per Wiki: practice for collaboration and communication between data scientists and operations professionals to help manage production ML lifecycle.

2. AI-OPS

Gartner predicts that large enterprise exclusive use of AIOps and digital experience monitoring tools to monitor applications and infrastructure will rise from 5% in 2018 to 30% in 2023.

AIOps is a nomenclature used for using complicated infrastructure monitoring and also cloud remedy tracking devices to *automate the data analysis* as well as regular DevOps procedures. The major defect of system monitoring devices constructed ten and even five years back is that they were not built to meet the needs of Big Data.

They also cannot take care of the sheer volume of the inbound information, have the ability to process all the selection of the data types, or remain on par with the velocity of the data input. Generally of thumb, such cloud surveillance services have to divide the information right into portions, different what is apparently vital and removed what is seemingly unwanted, operating with focus teams and statistical examples rather of taking care of the entire integrity of data.

The essential outcome is that some vital patterns may be left unseen as well as completely omitted from the photo on the data visualization phase of data analysis. This renders the entire procedure utterly worthless, as if Big Information analysis cannot produce workable business understandings, it cannot deliver the Fourth and essential point of Big Data-- Worth.

AIOps Enters the Scene

Handling all the inbound machine-generated data on time is not humanly feasible, naturally. However, this is specifically the type of task Artificial Knowledge (AI) formulas like Deep Knowing designs excel at. The only staying concern is the following: how to place this Artificial intelligence (ML) tools to great work in the life of DevOps designers?

Right here is just how AIOps can assist your IT division:

- *Process the data rapidly.* An ML design can be educated to refine all kinds of data produced by your systems-- and also it will certainly do so in the future. If a brand-new type of data should be included-- a version can be relatively easily readjusted and retrained, keeping the all-time performance high. This will certainly make certain data integrity as well as integrity, leading to a thorough analysis and concrete results.

- *In-depth data evaluation.* When all the data is assessed, the hidden patterns arise, and also workable insights offer themselves.

The DevOps engineers can, after that, identify the demand for infra adjustments to circumvent the performance bottlenecks and can have a place at the C-suite table with details data-based recommendations for facilities optimization as well as operations improvement.

- *Automation of routine tasks.* When the event patterns are determined, automated triggers can be set. Therefore stated, when the statistics show that particular events constantly result in a particular (unfavorable) outcome as well as specific actions have to be executed to remedy the issue, DevOps engineers can develop the triggers and also *automate the reactions to such events.*

Therefore if a surveillance service reports the raised CPU usage as a result of an enhanced number of links, etc., Kubernetes can rotate up the added application circumstances and also make use of the lots balancing to distribute the site visitor circulation and also reduce the lots.

This is the most basic circumstance, real-world use instances are much extra complex and enable to automate essentially any kind of routine DevOps task, enabling the ML design to launch it under certain conditions and deal with the problems preemptively, not after a downtime takes place.

Deploying AIOps allows achieving the following positive results:

- *Continuous product schedule,* causing a positive end-user experience

- *Preemptive issue solving,* as opposed to long-term firefighting

- *Elimination of information silos* as well as root-cause removal, because of the analysis of all the data your organization creates rather of working with disrobed samples

- *Automation of routine tasks,* allowing your IT division to concentrate on boosting the framework and also processes, as opposed to taking care of repetitive as well as lengthy jobs

- *Better cooperation*, as the comprehensive evaluation of the logs assists, show the impact of managerial decisions as well as review the effectiveness of adopted business methods

Ideas on What AIOps is and also why it is necessary

As you can see, deciding for AIOps tools and also services can be substantially advantageous for your organization. It may look like a marketing strategy of AIOps remedy vendors, yet there are none as of yet. The late majority of businesses is having problem with their change to DevOps society as well as performing their electronic transformation.

At the very same time, the innovative business are already applying their initiatives to integrating AI algorithms, ML models, as well as DevOps systems to provide the advanced cloud monitoring and also facilities automation solutions of tomorrow. Applying these practices results in greatly far better customer experience, shorter time to market for the products, a lot more efficient framework use as well as much better cooperation within the group.

Nevertheless, also these trendsetters do not have an out-of-the-box option readily available for their needs and also have to develop such systems themselves, making use of popular DevOps tools like Kubernetes, Splunk, Sumologic, Datadog, Prometheus, Grafana, and Terraform, etc. What is more vital, while the idea itself is of excellent significance, the degree of facilities administration skills required to apply it by much goes beyond the abilities of a typical business.

Artificial Intelligence to increase DevOps Efficiency

Over the last few years, Agile and also DevOps have increased the rate of software delivery. Any more decreases in time to market might lead to significant advantages against rivals. Ways to fine-tune efficiency remain in high demand, and also for many designers, the future hinge on using Artificial Intelligence to understand efficiency gains throughout the product delivery lifecycle. In no higher than a few years' time, Agile has actually become the leading methodology in the software world.

It really did not take much time before item developers in all industries recognized that using quickly, iterative as well as step-by-step approaches wouldn't jeopardize top product quality, however, could significantly decrease delivery times. Today, Agile is a de-facto standard method, and early adopters have long carried on to executing DevOps techniques to additional accelerate as well as improve the continual advancement of their software.

Like so lots of various other markets, software application development seems to have actually reached a factor of maturity where the method onward remains in maximizing performance. Rather than advanced concepts, a business can currently stay in advance of the curve by grasping Agile and also DevOps techniques to shave important job hrs off their distribution procedures. An exciting location of technology checks out the use of Artificial Intelligence to offer such benefits.

Artificial Intelligence for Agile/DevOps

The reason to the success of DevOps is making use of automation to cut the time and initiative expenses of particular software advancement procedures. So, wide variety of relatively basic and also commonly recurring jobs, wise approaches to automate can help understand fantastic efficiencies in the CI/CD pipeline. With AI, the array of jobs that can be automated is substantially increased, and also its usage cases extend past that.

There are several possible opportunities for using machine learning and also AI in software growth. The Software application's method, targeting predictive development, entails using Artificial Intelligence to enable accurate projections on numerous stages of the software program delivery lifecycle.

Predictive approaches use machine learning to historical information collections, making it possible for the velocity as well as improved precision of preparation, effort estimate, advancement, testing, as well as manufacturing. With transfer learning, these predictive algorithms can then be related to virtually any type of information collection. By doing this, AI has the possibility to positively impact every phase of software application delivery, speeding up the entire process.

"Transfer learning is a ML concept where a model created for a job is reused as the beginning point for a model on a second task."

Software application's AI idea

By extracting useful information from all that information, Artificial Intelligence can make projections on future projects to assist decision-making.

The principle on used machine learning could, for circumstances, judge the state of an existing sprint and also anticipate future efficiency without a retrospective evaluation of anti-patterns. Counting on the processing of story factor information by an AI algorithm, the option can anticipate future patterns on your burn down trajectory.

In impact, any AI component will certainly have the ability to advise scrum masters early in the situation. It "assumes" that the current sprint's deadline could be at risk. By having access to these details well beforehand, scrum masters will certainly be able to alter their source allotment decisions to see to it the sprint is ended up in a timely manner.

In a similar way, AI algorithm will have the ability to analyze historic group velocity data and tell you the anticipated average rate of your groups. This will significantly sustain efforts to optimize the dimension of sprint backlogs, and also can help grasp agile shipment by likewise discovering resource restrictions.

In general, the application of anticipating Artificial Intelligence-based algorithms in the growth of facility software can aid speed up Agile/DevOps distribution. By making use of machine learning to draw insights from large quantities of lifecycle data, AI attributes will make it possible for far better capability preparation, boosted item quality, and a lower overall risk degree.

AI comes to DevOps pipeline through containerization.

Developing applications for the cloud today leads to containerized microservices. And also, significantly, artificial intelligence (AI) -- based in machine-learning (ML) versions-- goes to the core of those cloud applications.

Development tool vendors have actually recognized the need to develop and deploy containerized AI/ML designs within cloud applications. They have actually responded by the structure in support for containerization-- specifically, within Docker images that are orchestrated via Kubernetes. They likewise support configuring these applications using languages such as Python, Java, and R.

What application programmers and also IT specialists require to recognize concerning what AI is, exactly how it connects to DevOps, and just how containerization allows DevOps pipelines to deploy AI applications into cloud-computing atmospheres. Also as we examine one new open-source tool, *Kubeflow*, and talk about exactly how to integrate AI-based DevOps tools as well as jobs right into existing continuous integration/continuous deployment (CI/CD) atmospheres.

Why we need AI intervention in DevOps pipeline.

AI is at the core of application these days and also data researchers are crucial programmers in this brand-new globe. A lot more programmers have begun to incorporate AI-- in some cases called ML or deep learning (DL) -- right into their cloud solutions initiatives.

AI is everything about making use of artificial neural network algorithms to infer correlations and also patterns in datasets. When integrated right into statistical designs and used to automate the purification of understandings from large data, AI can accomplish excellent outcomes. Common applications include predictive analysis, e-commerce referral engines, embedded mobile chatbots, automated face recognition, image-based search, and also others.

AI adoption can get made complex

To be efficient at their designated jobs, AI-infused cloud apps call for even more than simply the right data to construct and also train these versions. Any organization that wishes to harness AI has likewise to have programmers that have actually understood the tools and the abilities of data science. Additionally, a lasting AI development method calls for the adoption of mysterious approaches, high-performance computing collections, and complex processes into enterprise development methods.

Progressively, ventures are straightening their AI development exercise with their existing venture DevOps methods. This enables AI designs to be developed, deployed, as well as repeated in the very same CI/CD setting as the program code, application programming interfaces (APIs), individual experience layouts, and various other application artifacts.

Within DevOps procedures, data researchers are the ones that construct, educate, and examination AI models versus actual data in the application domain name of interest. This guarantees that the resulting applications are suitable for the objectives for which they have actually been built.

AI developers likewise should maintain re-evaluating as well as retraining their versions versus fresh data over an application's life. This guarantees that the models can remain to do their work-- such as acknowledging faces, Predicting events, as well as presuming client intents-- with appropriate accuracy.

The tools you'll need

Within a CI/CD practice, the DevOps atmosphere ought to automate AI pipeline activities to the maximum extent possible throughout the application lifecycle. This needs financial investment in numerous important platforms and tools.

-Source-control repository

This is where you save, manage, and also control all designs, code, as well as various other AI pipeline artifacts through every action of the DevOps lifecycle. The repository works as the center for collaboration, reuse, and sharing of all pipeline artifacts by all included development as well as procedures professionals.

-Data Lake
This is where you save, accumulated, and prepare data for use in exploration, modeling, as well as training throughout the AI DevOps pipeline. Normally, the data lake is a distributed file system, such as Hadoop, that stores multi-structured data in its original formats to assist in data exploration, modeling, as well as training by AI programmers.

-Integrated partnership setting
This is the workbench in which AI DevOps professionals perform all or most pipeline functions. It provides a unified system for source discovery, visualization, exploration, data prep work, statistical modeling, training, deployment, assessment, sharing, as well as reuse. The majority of embed prominent AI modeling structures such as TensorFlow, Caffe, PyTorch, and Mxnet.

-Embrace containerization in your AI development
Establishing AI applications for the cloud needs developing this functionality into containerized microservices. This involves using Python, Java, and various other languages to integrate AI as well as various other application reasoning right into Docker pictures that can be orchestrated using Kubernetes or other cloud-services orchestration backbones.

For successfully establishing AI microservices, developers need to factor the underlying application capacities into modular building blocks that can be released into cloud-native environments with marginal binding among sources. In a cloud services setting, you containerize and coordinate AI microservices dynamically within lightweight interoperability fabrics.

Generally, each containerized AI microservice reveals an independent, programmable API, which enables you to conveniently recycle, progress, or change it without jeopardizing interoperability. Each containerized AI microservice might be implemented utilizing different program languages, formula collections, cloud databases, and various others making it possible for back-end infrastructure.

AI DevOps tools are involving market in droves

To deal with these demands in repeatable DevOps pipelines, business development groups are adopting a brand-new generation of data science development workbenches. These incorporate CI/CD performance as well as integrate with existing enterprise financial investments in large data, HPC (High performance computing) platforms and also various other necessary facilities.

Business AI DevOps devices originate from public cloud service providers, including Alibaba Cloud, Amazon.com Internet Solutions, Microsoft, Google, IBM, and Oracle. AI tools are additionally available from well-known large data analytics remedy vendors, including Alteryx, Cloudera, Databricks, KNIME, MapR, Micro Focus, Nvidia, RapidMiner, as well as SAS Institute.

Likewise, there is a large range of specialized start-ups in this market sector, consisting of Pipeline.ai, PurePredictive, Seldon, Tellmeplus, Weaveworks, DataKitchen, DataRobot, Domino Data Lab, H2O.ai, Agile Stacks, Anaconda, Hydrosphere.io, Kogentix, ParallelM, , and also Xpanse AI.

Kubeflow's spot in this world

Progressively, the tools give the capacity to release containerized AI microservices over Kubernetes orchestration backbones that extend public, exclusive, hybrid, multi-cloud and even side environments.

Recognizing the demand for standards in this regard, the AI community has, in the past year, coalesced around an open-source task that automates the AI DevOps pipeline over Kubernetes collections. Introduced by Google in late 2017, Kubeflow gives a framework-agnostic pipe for making AI microservices production-ready across multi-framework, multi-cloud computer environments.

Kubeflow sustains the whole DevOps lifecycle for containerized AI. It streamlines the creation of production-ready AI microservices, makes certain the flexibility of containerized AI apps amongst Kubernetes clusters, and also supports scaling of AI DevOps workloads to any kind of cluster size.

It's created to support any type of work in the end-to-end AI DevOps pipe, varying from up-front data prep work to modeling as well as training, right to downstream serving, analysis, and also monitoring of containerized AI microservices.

Yet Kubeflow is far from fully grown and has been adopted only in a handful of commercial AI workbench as well as DevOps product offerings. Early adopters of Kubeflow include Agile Stacks, Alibaba Cloud, Amazon.com Internet Solutions, Google, H20.ai, IBM, NVIDIA, and Weaveworks.

How to get going

Establishing AI apps for containers in the cloud requires expert personnel, advanced tooling, scalable cloud systems, and efficient DevOps operations. To evaluate, business application development, as well as procedures experts that wish to bring AI development totally into their cloud-computing campaigns, must hearken the complying with recommendations:

- Align your AI application development exercise with your existing enterprise DevOps approaches. This will certainly permit you to construct, release and also iterate ML, DL, as well as various other statistical models in the exact same APIs setting interfaces, user experience layouts, and also various other application artifacts.

- Offer AI application DevOps teams with a shared collaboration workbench. This will permit data prep work, statistical modeling, training, implementation, as well as the refinement of versions, code, APIs, containerized microservices, and other development artifacts.

- Make certain that your AI DevOps operations sustain continuous re-training of released AI designs against fresh data over an application's life. This will make certain that AI-infused applications proceed to do their marked tasks-- such as recognizing faces, predicting occasions, as well as inferring consumer intents-- with appropriate precision.

- Manage the AI DevOps process from a resource control repository. This will certainly serve as the center for collaboration, versioning, recycle, and also sharing of all pipeline artifacts by all individuals.

Most important of all, bring data researchers completely right into your application development companies and DevOps techniques. They are competent professionals that have the knowledge to construct, train, test, release, and also manage AI designs that are anchored in the real data in the application domain names of passion.

AI in DevOps- Use Instances

DevOps isn't a new idea; IT groups all over the world have adopted its concepts for years now. Nonetheless, given the speed at which processes, modern technologies, and tools are developing, it's ending up being increasingly tough to cope with properly implementing DevOps principles. Besides, companies are increasing the pressure on their IT teams, demanding even more continuity in combination and also delivery-- at the click of a switch.

As CI/CD at scale in real-time comes to be significantly more difficult to accomplish, the most effective option to keep up is Data Science. Right here are some used cases where the addition of Machine Learning the mix will aid the DevOps cause profoundly.
Track application shipment

Activity data from DevOps tools (such as JIRA, Git, Jenkins, SonarQube, Puppet, Ansible, etc.) gives presence right into the full application distribution procedure. You can make use of machine learning to discover abnormalities in that data-- huge code volumes, long construct times, slow-moving release prices, late code check-ins-- to find most of the 'wastes' of the software application development.

Review software application testing performance

Artificial intelligence can examine QA outcomes and recognize unique errors by assessing the outcome from testing devices. As an example, ML algorithms can give details on typical or regular flaws, as well as malfunction predictions or patterns.

Safe and secure application delivery

You can apply Machine Learning to examine the individual practices of the DevOps group as well as determine abnormalities that may stand for dangerous activities.

The best goal of DevOps is total automation throughout the project lifecycle. While full automation is a remote truth in the meantime, we can make every effort to automate as high as possible, as well as not just within a solitary phrase or tool.

We use AI to eliminate information silos within the tool chain, which produces a conducive setting to automate evaluation, log as well as metric data. Eg Connection of all relevant data within a tool chain. The benefits of automation consist of greater speed, even more accurate origin evaluation, and anticipating understandings that are gotten from the whole tool chain, as opposed to simply one specific tool or data source.

Raised Collaboration

Collaboration is a keystone (and a vital one, at that) of the DevOps paradigm. It is vital for there to be a free flow of information concerning the ideal method to run applications as well as systems, between the IT, design, and also procedures teams. This, in turn, implies seamless interaction and cooperation.

We can make use of AI for cooperation within a DevOps team by giving a solitary sight to all project stakeholders, from which pertinent toolchain information can be accessed. AI likewise catches knowledge as it is created, concerning exactly how systems and also applications need to run. ML algorithms then display this expertise at times they are needed, for, e.g., when signals or abnormalities are discovered.

Software application documentation
Documentation is hard to preserve, as well as the need to be continually updated. AI could also play a huge duty in software documentation. The exact same sort of natural language processing used by Google to automate news writing could be made use of to document attribute adjustment checklists, API technical details, and also procedures utilized by DevOps groups.

Pattern exploration
Pattern discovery in logs provides an extremely reliable as well as automated means of discovering new knowledge in logs and thus making ultimately monotonous and also routine logs into actions. For instance, a log file could be discovered to have a duplicating pattern of connections from a relatively diverse collection of source IP addresses. When presented, this pattern may be taken as a new exploitation tool, discreetly tried out a firm network. It can then cause a collection of actions by a safety team and also the community at big.

Evaluation of fads as well as a recap
Recaps and trends are a common outcome of log analysis. Long log documents could be summed up into a brief "Top 10 Attacks" or "Leading Suspicious IP Addresses" or an unlimited number of various other beneficial recaps. Typically, such recap sight will certainly trigger an action. For instance, it could become obvious from a "Top Bandwidth Users" report that the top 3 users in the business use 90% of readily available bandwidth.

This can rapidly bring about a disciplinary activity, particularly if such bandwidth is used to share files on P2P or to download and install non-work related products. In a similar way, monitoring of a router CPU use log over a lengthy period of time could disclose periods of the abnormally high task, resulting in an examination possibly

finding aggressor interaction with a jeopardized system.
AI in DevOps is a brand-new as well as an interesting application of Data Science, and one that we're actively tracking. Remain tuned to our blog site for even more!

Basic Concepts: Cut the Clutter

DevOps is a software application development method that pairs software application growth (Dev) in addition to IT procedures (Ops) to quicken the application development life cycle while distributing functions, updates, and bug solutions in a compelling fashion that lines up with service goals.

MLOps refers to the cooperation between data scientists as well as IT operations specialists to help manage the manufacturing machine finding out lifecycle.

AIOps refers to software program systems that couple huge data as well as AI performance to boost and possibly replace a wide variety of IT processes such as efficiency monitoring, accessibility surveillance, occasion evaluation, IT services management, and also automation.

How to start AIOPS in the existing setup?

Do not wait. End up being acquainted with AI and also ML vocabulary and capabilities today, even if an AIOps project isn't imminent. Concerns and also capabilities adjustment, so you may require it sooner than you expect.

Select initial test cases carefully. Initial changes are not often profitable. Increase expertise, and repeat from there. Take the same technique to integrate AIOps for success.

Experiment easily. Although AIOps systems are of high cost and also intricacy, a good deal of open-source and also low-cost ML software is offered to allow you to assess AIOps as well as data science applications and uses.

Look past IT. Take advantage of data and analytics sources that may already be existing in your company. Information administration is a substantial element of AIOps, as well as teams, are frequently currently knowledgeable. Service analytics, as well as statistical evaluation, are key parts of any contemporary organization.

Standardize where possible: improve where practical. Prepare your infrastructure to support an eventual AIOps application by taking on a constant automation style, infrastructure as code (IaC) as well as immutable infrastructure patterns.

3. ML-OPS

The Next Generation of DevOps: ML Ops

· Mar 2018

The story of enterprise Machine Learning: "It took me 3 weeks to develop the model. It's been >11 months, and it's still not deployed." @DineshNirmalIBM #StrataData #strataconf

7   22

A Tweet with Real World problem

The age of AI is upon us. As AI ends up being much more common, several are discovering new and also cutting-edge means to operationalised data science to raise efficiency, rate, and range.

As we consider typical DevOps methodologies, there are harmonies as well as parallels that can additionally be put on the data science globe. The brand-new chasm includes several techniques: *Data Engineering, Data Science, as well as Software Program Design.*

Typical DevOps is the battleground for designers and also procedures that proceeds worldwide of data science in a much more noticeable fashion-- data engineers, data scientists, software program developers, and procedures. These four identities featured different demands, restrictions, and velocity. It is extremely tough to balance all four that please the business requirements while conforming to corporate as well as business plans.

The Rise of ML Ops

Ideal data design is required to transform *raw data right into processed data proper for use in machine learning algorithms.* This results in a fusion of data design and also data science, and also otherwise done properly, impact *productivity, efficiency, and also speed advancement, deployment, and also eventually broad adoption of data science.*

We call this "ML Ops," an essential element of machine learning advancement that enhances and also finishes the *life cycle of an ML designer.*

ML Ops encapsulates aspects of *data design, software application engineering, and also data science* to provide an *end-to-end view of applying intelligence from data to a business use instance.*

A majority of data science projects remain in the laboratories due to the fact that combination with production environments is extremely complicated, manual as well as prone to error. The lack of advanced ML Ops for that reason impedes any type of company or business to remove knowledge from the data they already have and apply them to their business processes and triggers disillusionment of data science as well as machine learning in general.

We are beginning to see automation frameworks, and also solutions emerge in the general public and personal domain name that bridge the ability and also procedure voids of data science, software program growth, and also data design.

Using ML Ops to Your Company

An ML Ops platform will provide end-to-end automation of the processes that involve *fixing a service problem.*

A regular automation procedure includes repetitive life process in data engineering (prep work, cleansing, refining and also transformation), data science (version development, training, testing, validation, and optimization) and also releases (further screening, implementation, trial and error, tracking, efficiency design as well as operating).

Each of these is really complex procedures as well as have different devices and systems that normally don't integrate well, include great deals of manual touch factors and also handoffs and also occasionally don't even interoperate. The first order of trouble is the absence of visibility as well as openness in the end-to-end process. A modern ML ops engineering platform will certainly *sew together these disparate steps into smooth operations* that will allow partnership between everybody associated with solving a business problem.

We are in the really beginning of *"Data Science Performance,"* comparable to the days when the initial devices like compilers or editors began to appear for establishing software program for computers. We see 2 key factors for an absence of integrated devices as well as platforms in this room:

a) The quickly changing landscape in each of the three contributing areas: data systems, data science algorithms and also platforms, and also cloud infrastructure

b) Skill as well as ability voids in thoroughly comprehending all the disciplines involved to be able to give meaningful abstraction, automation and efficiency in a common style that is broadly appropriate and also useful to a lot of genuine functional usage cases.

The essential need of the hour is to be able to provide as well as use quality intelligence that can be depended on business trouble rapidly. There is a remarkable demand for refreshing the designs in near real-time, otherwise real-time. On top of that, the business intends to experiment with a selection of intelligence for enhancing the client's experience, which implies applying a various sample of data, model as well as a software program. Lack of top quality as well as for this reason testing in this entire cycle diminishes count on and also the repeatability of the outcomes. In lots of sectors, like banking as well as insurance coverage, there is a governing need for showing reproducibility and veracity of the design utilizing the exact same data. And consequently, the ability to supply abilities to test during the development, implementation, and also article usage is incredibly vital for both efficiencies as well as compliance.

As the encapsulation of Data Science with Data comes to be more sophisticated, we can anticipate providing AI as well as machine learning in an exceptionally scalable fashion via several cloud solutions.

Real ML Ops driven end-to-end data science platform can have *a transformative impact on the globe by unlocking the hidden knowledge in all of the data existing in each service and also in the public domain.*

DevOps for Machine Learning

Both data science, as well as data design issues, need to be solved in alongside allow data scientists to be successful. Because the Machine Learning stack is developed to automate the intricacy of machine learning pipes, data scientists have even more time to concentrate on the modeling jobs.

DevOps automation for ML permits speeding up the process through which an idea goes from advancement to production. It helps to achieve several crucial objectives:

- Lowest time to train, with as much data than and also as properly as feasible

- Fastest time to reasoning, with the ability to swiftly re-train

- Safe and reliable releases to observe model behavior in the real globe

An additional area of automation that is resolved by Machine Learning stack is experiment monitoring and also model versioning.

Releasing machine learning systems to production generally calls for the capacity to run lots of models and numerous variations of models at similar timings. The code, data preparation workflows, and models can be easily versioned in Git, and also data collections can be versioned via cloud storage space (AWS S3, Minion, Ceph etc.). Version control basically empowers us to concurrently run multiple versions of models to maximize results, as well as rollback to previous versions when needed.

As opposed to ad-hoc scripts, we can now use Git push/pull commands to move consistent plans of ML models, data, as well as code into Dev, Test, as well as Production atmospheres.

The Agile Stacks Control Plane offers to function with each other on machine learning jobs. It simplifies the procedure of creating machine learning pipelines, data processing pipes, as well as integrates AI/Machine Learning with existing applications and also service procedures.

A common Machine Learning pipeline consists of a number of actions:

1. Data prep work/ ETL
2. Model training as well as screening
3. Model evaluation and validation
4. Implementation as well as versioning
5. Production and also surveillance
6. Continuous training

At the heart of Machine Learning Stack is the open resource Kubeflow system, improved and automated utilizing Agile Stacks' own safety, tracking, CI/CD, process, and arrangement administration capabilities. *Kubeflow is a Google-led open resource project created to relieve some of the extra tiresome jobs connected with machine learning.* It assists with handling deployment of machine learning apps through the complete cycle of advancement, screening, as well as production while permitting resource scaling as demand boosts.

Machine Learning Layout
With Agile Stacks, you can make up several finest of type structures as well as devices to construct a stack design template as well as essentially define your very own recommendation style for Machine Learning. Stack services are readily available using basic magazine options and supply plug-and-play support for monitoring, logging, analytics, as well as testing devices. Stack layout can likewise be prolonged with extra solutions making use of import of customized automation scripts.

Stack Service	Description	Available Implementations
ML Platform	Deployments of machine learning workflows on Kubernetes simple, portable and scalable.	Kubeflow, Kubernetes

ML Frameworks	Supported machine learning and deep learning frameworks, toolkits, and libraries.	TensorFlow, Keras, Caffe, PyTorch
Storage Volume Managemen t	Manage storage for data sets), automatically deploying required storage implementations, and providing data backup	Local FS, AWS EFS, AWS EBS,Ceph (block and object), Minio,NFS, HDFS
Image Managemen t	Private Docker registry allows to secure and manage the distribution of container images.	Amazon ECR, Harbor Registry
Workflow Engine	Specify, schedule, and coordinate the running of containerized workflows and jobs on Kubernetes, optimized for scale and performance.	Argo
Model Training	Collaborative & interactive model training	JupyterHub, TensorBoard, Argo workflow templates
Model Serving	Export and deploy trained models on Kubernetes. Expose ML models via REST and gRPC for easy integration into business apps that need predictions.	Seldon, tf-serving
Model Validation	Estimate model skill while tuning model's hyper parameters. Compare desired outputs with model predictions	Argo workflow templates
Data Storage Services	Distributed data storage and database systems for structured and unstructured data	Minio, S3, MongoDB, Cassandra, HDFS

Data Preparation and Processing	Workflow application templates allow to create data processing pipelines to automatically build container images, ingest data, run transformation code, and schedule workflows	Argo, NATS, workflow
Infrastructure Monitoring	Monitor performance metrics, collect, visualize, and alert on all performance metric data using pre-configured monitoring tools	Prometheus, Grafana

Source: Agilestacks.com

Kubeflow Pipelines

Kubeflow Pipelines provide a workbench to make up the machine learning process, as well as plans ML code to make it multiple-use to other users across a company. It provides a workbench to *compose, release and take care of the machine learning process* that does orchestration of many parts: a learner for generating models based on training data, modules for model recognition, as well as facilities for offering models in production. Data scientists can also check a number of ML techniques to see which one works best for their application.

Machine Learning Pipe Templates

Machine Learning Pipelines play a vital role in building production-ready AI/ML systems. Utilizing ML pipelines, data scientists, data designers, as well as IT operations can collaborate on the steps associated with data preparation, model training, model recognition, model deployment, as well as model screening.

Agile Stacks Machine Learning pipe templates offer out of package implementation for common ML issues like NLP processing along with RNN (Recurrent Neural Network) sequence-to-sequence learning in Keras *(Keras is a neural network library)*, as well as the offering of models with Seldon *(Seldon is an open-source platform upon which data scientists and developers can leverage the core building blocks of machine learning)*.

The pipes enable to design of multi-step workflows as a series of jobs, where each step in the workflow is Python documents. Pipe actions can be implemented from the Jupyter note pad *(Jupyter Notebook is an open-source web application that allows you to create and share documents that contain live code)*for initial experiments or scaled throughout multiple GPUs for faster training on huge quantities of data. Data scientists can specify data preparation jobs, and also various other calculate intensive data processing jobs that can auto-scale across several Kubernetes containers. A very automated approach for data consumes as well as preparation permits to avoid data mistakes, rise velocity of iterating on new experiments, reduce technical, financial obligation, and also boost model accuracy.

Machine Learning pipes are utilized by data scientists to develop, enhance, as well as handle their end-to-end machine learning process.

For assisting with experiment monitoring, multiple workflows can be generated from a single layout. With distributed training, data scientists can attain a significant reduction in time to educate a deep learning model. Agile Stacks pipe design templates provide complete DevOps automation for ML pipelines. When data scientists are allowed with DevOps automation, the procedures team no more needs to supply setup monitoring and provisioning support for usual demands such as collection scale up as well as reduce, as well as the entire organization can become a lot more agile.

Continuous implementation of brand-new models in highly automated, as well as trusted way, is a trick for building progressed machine learning systems that integrate several models to supply the most effective precision, while regularly keeping an eye on model efficiency on real data.

Basic Concepts: Cut the Clutter

ML Pipeline: A machine learning pipeline is made to help automate machine learning operations. They operate by enabling a sequence of information to be changed and correlated with each other in a model that can be checked as well as evaluated to attain an outcome.

NLP: NLP stands for Neuro-Linguistic Programming. Neuro refers to your neurology; Linguistic refers to language; programming refers to just how that neural language functions. Simply put, finding out NLP is like learning the language of your own mind

ETL: ETL is short for extract, transform, load, three database features that are combined into one device to pull data out of one database as well as place it into one more database.

Docker: Docker is a containerization system that packages your application and all its dependences together in the type of a docker container to make certain that your application works seamlessly in any type of setting.

ML for Application: development course as well as a data science course.

Until very recently, a lot of companies have seen two distinct, non-overlapping work streams when developing an AI made it possible for application: *a development course as well as a data science course.*

Often, both groups are, in fact, constructing in a similar way scripted functional solutions making use of something like python or C/F #. Even more, as soon as a data researcher completes the examination and model choice action of the data science process, we have actually located there to be a "confusion vacuum cleaner" when it concerns ideal techniques around incorporating right into existing or boosting brand-new service procedures, each side not completely recognizing exactly how to support the various other/ when to involve. Much of the convergence, in my viewpoint, has been sustained by the growing appeal as well as the use of container solutions like Docker and also Kubernetes, especially in the DevOps world.

So, exactly how do these swim lanes converge, you ask? I'm delighted you did!

You can also develop a continuous integration pipeline for an AI application, for beginners.

The pipeline starts causing the test collection run(s). If the test passes, it takes the most up to date build, packages it right into a Docker container in addition to all essential bundles, and also package dependencies/ versions to run to design successfully.

The container is then deployed using a container solution held in the cloud, like @Azure Container Service (#ACS) as well as the subsequent pictures are securely stored in the connected container registry (#ACR). This is great for small scale or development objectives; however, when you require to operationalised or release to production-grade, you would after that look towards a service like Kubernetes for managing/ coordinating the container collections (other solution choices are #Docker-Throng/ #Mesos).

The application safely pulls the most current pertained #ML design from a cloud-based blob storage account as well as bundles that as part of the application. The released application has the application code, as well as ML model packaged as solitary container and the properties and outputs, become component of the signed-in code that gets pressed back right into your business code database for version control et al.

Using ML to DevOps

The globe is using static tooling for product packaging, provisioning, implementations, as well as surveillance, APM, and log monitoring, more than ever. With Docker fostering, the Cloud and API driven strategies and micro-services to releasing applications at a huge scale, making certain high reliability, calls for an outstanding take. So, it's important to include creative handling tools for the cloud rather than changing the wheel every single time. With the surge of ML and AI, a lot more DevOps tooling vendors are integrating intelligence with their offerings for additional simplifying the task of engineers.

The synergy between Machine Learning (ML) as well as DevOps is potent, and their related capabilities consist of:

- *IT Operations Analytics (ITOA).*
- *Predictive Analytics (PA).*
- *Artificial Intelligence (AI).*
- *Algorithmic IT Operations (AIOps).*

Machine Learning is the useful application of Artificial Intelligence (AI) in the type of a set of programs or algorithms. The aspect of finding out relies upon training time and data.

ML conceptually represents acceleration and codification of "Culture of Continuous Learning" by Gene Kim's. The teams can extract direct patterns, substantial complex datasets, and also antipatterns, and fine-tune inquiries, uncover brand-new understandings, as well as continuously repeat all at the rate of a computer system.

ML is coming to be popular in software and applications, as well as in all sectors, from accounting to other utility apps. When any one of these ML strategies is contributed to interesting projects, it causes some difficulties.

ML frequently increases the objective of applications that remain in presence, including web store recommendations, category of utterances in a chatbot, etc. It will certainly be a part of the substantial cycle with brand-new added functions, dealing with bugs or other factors for constant modifications in general code.

Also, ML can exist in lots of methods the following generation of Automation. DevOps with Automation makes it possible for a fast SDLC, yet one that is too distributed, vibrant, opaque, and ephemeral for the understanding of the human. Similar to Automation, ML distinctly manages the quantity, velocity, as well as variety of information that is created, making use of new delivery procedures and also utilizing the next-generation of atomized, composable, and scaled out applications.

Applying Machine Learning to DevOps

There is effective synergy between DevOps and Machine Learning (ML) -- and also relevant capabilities, like Predictive Analytics, IT Operations Analytics (ITOA), Mathematical IT Operations (AIOps), as well as Artificial Intelligence (AI).

Conceptually, *ML stands for codification and also the acceleration of Gene Kim's "Culture of Continuous Learning."* With ML DevOps, groups can mine large complex datasets, identify patterns as well as antipatterns, reveal brand-new understandings, repeat and fine-tune queries, and also repeat regularly-- all at 'computer system speed.'

Similarly, ML remains in lots of ways the next-generation of Automation, structure on John Willis' as well as Damon Edwards' prescription for 'CAMERAS.' With Automation, DevOps allows a much faster SDLC, yet one that is as well opaque, dispersed, vibrant, as well as transient for regular human comprehension. However, like Automation, ML distinctly handles the rate, quantity, and also range of information generated by brand-new delivery procedures and also the next-generation of composable, atomized, as well as scale-out applications.

In the method, some key examples of applying ML to DevOps consist of:

Tracking application delivery

Task information from 'DevOps tools' (like Jira, Git, Jenkins, SonarQube, Puppet, Ansible, etc.) provides exposure to the delivery procedure. Applying ML can uncover anomalies in that data-- big code volumes, long develop times, sluggish launch rates, late code check-ins-- to recognize a lot of the 'wastes' of software program advancement, including gold-plating, partial work, ineffective resourcing, extreme job changing, or process slowdowns.

Making sure the application top quality

By analyzing results from testing tools, ML can wisely examine QA outcomes, find unique errors, and properly construct an examination pattern collection based upon exploration.

This machine-driven understanding of a 'recognized good launch' aids to make sure thorough screening on every launch, even for unique defects, raising the quality of supplied applications.

Protecting application delivery

Patterns of user behavior can be as one-of-a-kind as fingerprints. Using ML to Dev as well as Ops user behaviors can aid in determining anomalies that may represent destructive activity. For instance, strange patterns of access to delicate repos, automation routines, deployment task, test execution, system provisioning, and much more can swiftly highlight individuals were exercising 'known poor' patterns-- whether intentionally or mistakenly-- such as coding back doors, releasing unapproved code, or stealing intellectual property.

Managing production

Examining an application in production is where machine learning really enters into its own due to the greater information quantities, user matters, purchases, and so on that occur in prod, compared to dev or examine. DevOps teams can make use of ML to evaluate 'regular' patterns-- customer quantities, resource application, transaction throughput, and so on-- as well as subsequently to spot 'irregular' patterns (e.g., DDOS problems, memory leakages, race conditions, etc.).

68

Handling alert tornados

A basic, practical, high-value use ML is in handling the enormous flood of informs that happen in production systems. This can be as basic as ML organizing relevant notifies (e.g., by a typical purchase ID; a typical set of web servers; or a typical subnet). Or it can be extra complex, such as 'training' systems gradually to acknowledge 'recognized good' and also 'recognized negative' alerts. This enables filtering to reduce sharp storms and alert exhaustion.

Troubleshooting and triage analytics

This is one more location where today's ML modern technologies radiate. ML can automatically spot and also begin to intelligently triage 'known problems,' as well as also some unidentified ones. As an example, ML devices can find abnormalities in 'regular' handling, and afterward, additionally, analyze release logs to correlate this problem with a new arrangement or deployment. Various other automation tools can utilize ML to alert procedures, open a ticket (or a conversation home window), as well as designate it to the right resource. In time, ML might even be able to suggest the ideal fix!

Preventing production failings

ML can work out past straight-line capacity planning in preventing failings. ML can map known good patterns of application to predict, for instance, the most effective arrangement for a preferred degree of performance; the number of customers will make use of a new attribute; framework demands for a brand-new promo; or exactly how an interruption will certainly affect consumer involvement. ML sees otherwise opaque 'very early indications' in systems and applications, allowing Ops to start removal or avoid problems, much faster than typical feedback times.

Evaluating organization influence

Recognizing the impact of code release on service objectives is critical to success in DevOps. By synthesizing and assessing real individual metrics, ML systems can find excellent and poor patterns to offer an 'early warning system' to coders and service groups alike when applications are having troubles (e.g., through very early coverage of increased cart desertion or foreshortened buyer journeys); or being extremely successful (e.g. through early discovery of high customer registrations or click-through rates).

Of training course, there is no easy button for ML, yet. There is no alternative to intelligence, experience, imagination, and a difficult job. Yet we are currently seeing a lot of this applied today, and also, as we continue to press the limits, the sky is the restriction.

The State of Machine Learning in DevOps

DevOps approaches are progressively creating significant as well as diverse data collections throughout the whole application lifecycle-- from development, to release, to application performance administration, and only a durable tracking and also evaluation layer can genuinely harness this data for the utmost DevOps objective of end-to-end automation.

The recent surge of machine learning-- as well as relevant capacities such as predictive analytics as well as artificial intelligence-- has actually begun to push companies to check out the implementation of a brand-new data evaluation design that counts on mathematical algorithms. Regardless of the promised advantage, helpful groups maximize operations and also obtain even more exposure right to their data, adoption of machine learning into the DevOps toolbox is restricted.

How Machine Learning Can Assist

Let's start by recognizing exactly how machine learning can suit and also profit the DevOps methodology. There are two crucial interrelated advantages for carrying out machine learning in DevOps: *decreasing the noise-to-signal ratio as well as replacing the reactive setting with an aggressive approach based on accurate forecasts.*

As a result of the way systems have been checked for years currently and also since a far better technique has actually not been presented yet, many teams today use the threshold method in monitoring. Limits are specified based upon conventional wisdom, gut feelings, as well as behavior.

If you have specified 50% CPU as the threshold for your EC2 instances, as well as this metric rises to 70%, your auto-scaling team will supply more circumstances up until the whole team goes back down to 50%.

This is obviously a substantial enhancement compared to the previous approach in the standard datacenter atmosphere, which was to link new web servers regularly.

The machine learning technique is grounded in a much more mathematical approach, specifying limits based upon what is statistically substantial as well as rationally sound. Machine learning uses different methods and versions, such as linear and also logistic regression, category, as well as deep learning, to check huge sets of data, identify patterns and also relationships, as well as make predictions.

The Present State of Machine Learning in DevOps

An increasing number of next-generation devices in the

DevOps stack support machine learning somewhat or various other, but the tools are often black boxes running as separated data silos.

With DevOps teams' still too active producing fires, and with a lack of DevOps specialists who genuinely recognize machine learning, predictive analytics, and AI, the overall effect of these devices on detailed and data-driven automation is still restricted.

Tracking or deployment items that do attribute machine learning normally do not provide presence right into exactly how the underlying formulas job, leaving data scientists cynical regarding whether its conclusions are appropriate. The black box strategy additionally runs counter to typical machine learning treatments that allow the expert to change the algorithm in an iterative style until it ends up being adequately exact.

Moreover, and perhaps more notably, also when the vendor does supply exposure, readjusting the machine learning to the company's requirements calls for expertise that average programmers do not have.

DevOps designers today are called to recognize how the facilities work, exactly how to code, as well as just how to utilize DBaaS in the cloud. Adding machine learning to this capability is a big, if not difficult challenge, since most DevOps designers are just not mathematicians.

Barrier # 1-- The Machine Learning Skills Space

Machine learning is used in mathematics. To comprehend it, the designer needs a solid understanding of logarithms, calculus, infinite series and also sequences, straight algebra, statistics, straight programming, regression evaluation, and trigonometry. Many college graduates studied these in university; however, they have actually most likely neglected them because they do not utilize them every day. Big data designers recognize collections and also how to run MapReduce functions. However, having drawn out as well as changed data, they could not know where to go from there to attract final thoughts and also make forecasts.

To do so, they require knowing what analytical feature and algorithm they need to make use of. Should they use logistic or linear regression, k-means clustering, assistance vector machines, naive Bayes, stochastic gradient descent, or a neural network? Every one of that lingo is indecipherable to the majority of. Understanding it, however, is what the data scientist does. A recent post in It is reported that in US due to being in such a brief supply, data scientists can gain approximately $300,000 each year.

Obstacle # 2-- Business Challenges

As mentioned previously, the number one challenge to integrating machine learning in a purposeful method right into DevOps is that routine computer system designers do not recognize used math and stats-- and machine learning is everything about data scientific research.

Consequently, a DevOps machine learning task will frequently have actually to be divided amongst various abilities and titles. Big Data designers, Big Data designers, Data Scientists-- assembling a multi-disciplinary group of this nature remain in itself a considerable business obstacle. Much more complicated is taking care of such a complex project to make sure that it satisfies its objectives on time and also within the spending plan. It's not unexpected.

Therefore, that including machine learning deeply into DevOps is not a simple choice for administration due to the fact that it certainly needs hiring new individuals and also compelling your present group to learn and control brand-new abilities.

Considering the Future

Despite the obstacles and also obstacles, machine learning adoption is only going to grow as high wages press even more IT designer's right into this space.

The primary reason for future development, though, is that formulas will certainly come to be easier to recognize as well as implement due to the proliferation of frameworks. Google, Facebook, and various other companies proceed to create and also hand out structures that enable data scientists and also Big Data designers to do more quickly what only a doctoral level researcher might do in the past.

Likewise, the database is growing as programmers devote what they have actually learned to brand-new open-source frameworks and make renovations to existing ones. Additionally, even more, individuals are becoming educated in these technologies as their usage rises, suggesting there is more make use of instances that people can refer to.

Although many DevOps suppliers have already included machine learning to their items, Logz.io consisted of; this does not exempt business from the demand to create their own machine learning code in order to optimize their automation capabilities. Offered the incredible benefits that a machine learning-driven DevOps infrastructure can bring to service procedures throughout the whole business, managers are currently taking actions to boost their team's machine learning coding and project administration expertise via hiring as well as training.

Exactly How to Enhance DevOps with Machine Learning

Among today's most prominent software development and also operations techniques, DevOps objectives to streamline as well as seamlessly incorporate software application designers and IT operations specialists to supply maximum value to the organization.

In the procedure of DevOps implementation, large quantities of data are produced that can be used to streamline operations, orchestration, tracking, troubleshooting, and also other tasks. The issue is that there is also much data. Server logs alone can gather numerous megabytes each week. If monitoring tools are made use of, then megabytes and also gigabytes of data are produced in a short duration of time.

The result is predictable: programmers do not examine the data as they are, yet they set limit values. So they are seeking exemptions as opposed to doing data analytics. However, also with the assistance of contemporary analytical tools, you still require to recognize what to try to find in your data collections.

The majority of the data created in the process of DevOps is related directly to the application release. Application tracking renews web server logs, creates error messages, and also purchase mapping. The only affordable way to test this data and make the right real-time conclusions is to make use of ML (Machine Learning).

ML can take some time before it is applied; if the algorithms and also network architectures are properly lined up, the machine learning system will certainly start producing the results that correspond to the real ones. Basically, the *neural network "learns" or models the connection between data as well as outcomes.* This model can, after that, be used to estimate future data.

ML as a rescue ranger for DevOps

Algorithms of machine evaluation, as well as learning, enable you to check details objects (e.g., data sources, applications, and so on) and construct the profiles of an adequate (errorless) system operation. In case of any type of variances (abnormalities), for instance, when the response time boosts, the application freezes or deals reduce down, the system records this situation and also sends a notification regarding it, which enables you to take procedures to stop such anomalies going ahead.

Just how challenging is it to educate such a system, the length of time does it take as well as just how many initiatives should be taken into it? Basically, no training is needed! The system learns itself on data collections without any programs requires, as well as can predict the partnership in-between data collections. It makes it feasible to stay clear of the "human aspect," therefore accelerating the system by removing hand-operated procedures (such as identification of data relationships, reliances, and so on).

The system establishes itself exactly how the objects ought to function adequately, and for additional modifications, parameterization mechanisms would certainly suffice. Nonetheless, although machine learning is an extremely effective tool, it requires building up data. Gradually, the variety of false positives reduces. You can also lower their number by slight "fine adjusting."

Changes systems aid make the algorithms much more exact, along with adjusting them to specific needs. Hence, over time, the accuracy improves because of the built-up stats.

Algorithmic approaches aim to identify abnormalities, clustering, and data relationship, as well as enhance the project. Do they assist in discovering a solution to numerous concerns like what is the source of trouble? Just how to avoid it? Is this behavior regular or abnormal? What can be improved in the application? What should I search for right away? Just how to stabilize the lots?
Regarding DevOps goes; ML can have numerous use situations.

Machine Learning Use Cases in DevOps

Application tracking

DevOps tools task data (for instance, Jira, Git, Jenkins, SonarQube, Puppet, Ansible, and so on) gives openness in the software application delivery procedure. Utilizing ML can reveal anomalies in this data such as huge amounts of code, long develop times, extended launch times and also code checks, as well as determine lots of "discrepancies" in software application development procedures, consisting of ineffective use of sources, frequent job changing, or reducing down the procedure.

Application high-quality assurance

By assessing the examination results, ML can assist in recognize new errors and produce a library of examination patterns based upon such exploration. This helps guarantee extensive screening of each launch, and enhance the top quality of the applications delivered (QA).

User actions patterns

Patterns of user behavior can be as special as fingerprints. Using ML behaviors to Dev and Ops can help recognize abnormalities that comprise destructive activity. This includes abnormal patterns of accessibility to crucial databases or users that intentionally or inadvertently make use of recognized "poor" patterns (for example, with backdoors), unauthorized code implementation, or theft of intellectual residential or commercial property.

Operation administration

Assessing an application throughout the operation is an area where machine learning can actually confirm itself because you need to manage large quantities of data, a massive number of customers, purchases, and so on. DevOps experts can make use of ML to evaluate customer habits, use of sources, throughput deal abilities, etc. for the objective of succeeding discovery of "unusual" patterns (for example, DDoS strikes, memory leakages, etc.).

Alert monitoring

Straightforward, as well as the practical use of ML, is to manage the mass flow of warnings (alarms) in the systems being run. This may be because of a typical purchase identifier, a usual collection of web servers, or a common subnet, or the factor is extra complex as well as needs systems to "discover" with time to identify "understood great" and also "known poor" cautions. This permits you to filter cautions.

Troubleshooting and analytics

This is an additional area where contemporary machine learning modern technologies perform well. ML can immediately detect as well as a sort of "recognized issues" and also even some unknown ones. For instance, ML tools can find anomalies in "typical" handling, and also, after that, better analyze the logs in order to associate this trouble to a brand-new arrangement or deployment. Various other automation tools can use ML to notify operations, open up a ticket number, and assign it to an appropriate person. Gradually, ML can even supply a better solution.

Stopping interruptions during operation

ML allows you to go far past basic resource planning to prevent system crashes. For instance, It can be utilized to anticipate the best configuration to achieve the desired level of efficiency, the number of customers who will use the new feature, infrastructure needs, etc. Early signs in systems and applications are seen by ML, allowing developers to make a strategy for mitigating any expected risks.

Business Impact Analysis

The understanding of the impact of code release on business goals is crucial for the success of DevOps culture. By analyzing the actual utilization rates, ML systems can find out good and bad models for implementing an "early warning system" when applications have issues. For example, ML can report the increased frequency of the shopping basket abandonment cases or certain impediments in the customer's journey.

Machine learning permits you to utilize large data sets and

helps make educated conclusions. Identifying statistically notable anomalies makes it feasible to recognize the erratic behavior of infrastructure objects. Also, ML makes it possible to identify not only various abnormalities in the processes but also the wrong action.

Recognizing and grouping records based on the common format helps you concentrate on data and cuts the background information. The analysis of the records preceding and following the error enhances the performance of locating the root causes of concerns, while the constant monitoring of applications for concern identification brings about their quick elimination during operation.

The following data kinds have a predictable format and are perfectly suited for ML: user data, diagnostics, and transaction data, metrics (e.g. of apps, virtual machines, containers, servers, etc.), infrastructure data, and so on.

Enhancing DevOps with ML

Regardless of whether you buy an industrial application or build it from scratch, there are several ways to utilize machine learning to enhance DevOps.

From thresholds to the predictive analytics, there is a great deal of data, DevOps specialists seldom see as well as examine the whole data set. Instead, they set limits, i.e., conditions for some activities. They dispose of the majority of the data collected and concentrate on deviations. Machine learning applications are capable of even more. They can be trained on all data, as well as while in run mode; these applications can watch the whole data streams and make conclusions. This will assist in using predictive analytics.

Look for trends, not mistakes: It follows from the above that, when picking up from all data, a machine learning system can show not just the issues identified. Analyzing data trends, DevOps professionals can determine what will certainly occur with time; that is, observe fads as well as make predictions.

Analysis as well as Correlation of Data Sets: Many of the data is a time collection, and one variable is very easy to trace. However, many patterns issue of several aspects. For instance, the response time might decrease when multiple purchases concurrently do the very same action. Such patterns are nearly challenging to find "with the naked eye" or with the help of traditional analytics. Yet properly educated applications will suit these relationships and patterns.

Historic data context: One of the most significant troubles in DevOps is to pick up from errors. Even if there is a strategy of continuous comments, then, probably, this is something like a Wikipedia, which describes the problems encountered, and what we did to examine them. A usual option is to reboot the webserver or reactivate the application. Machine learning systems can evaluate data and clearly show what took place yesterday, last week, month, or year. You can see seasonal or daily trends. At any moment, they will certainly offer us a real-life photo of your application's performance.

Correlation between tracking devices: In DevOps, several tools are commonly utilized concurrently to see as well as process data. Each of them manages the application performance in different means; however, it cannot find the partnership between this data from different devices. Machine learning systems can accumulate every one of these inconsonant data streams, utilize them as raw data, and create a much more precise and reliable photo of the

81

state of your application.

Orchestration effectiveness: If there are metrics for the orchestration procedure, machine learning can be used to determine how successful this orchestration is carried out.

Inadequacy can be the outcome of incorrect techniques or reduced orchestration, so researching these features can assist both in the option of devices and also in the organization of procedures.

Optimization of details metric: Are you looking to increase uptime? Keep the performance criteria? Or decrease the time in between releases? An adaptive machine learning system can help. Adaptive systems are systems without a particular answer or result. Their objective is to acquire input data and maximize particular attributes.

As an example, air ticket sales systems attempt to fill up in planes as well as maximize earnings by changing ticket rates up to three times a day. You can likewise maximize DevOps procedures. The neural network is educated to maximize (or reduce) the worth, instead of achieving a recognized outcome. This permits the system to alter its parameters throughout the operation in order to gradually accomplish the very best outcome.

Your supreme objective is to enhance, in a measurable way, DevOps techniques from idea to deployment and also decommissioning.

Implementing Docker, microservices, cloud modern technologies, and also APIs for releasing applications and also ensuring their high integrity requires brand-new approaches. Consequently, it is essential to utilize wise devices, so DevOps device suppliers integrate wise features into their items to further streamline and speed up software advancement procedures.

Of course, ML is no replacement for knowledge, experience, creative thinking, as well as effort. But we currently see adequate chances for its usage and also higher possibility in the future.

It is getting AI/ML and also DevOps working better with each other.

Artificial Intelligence (AI) and machine learning (ML) modern technologies extend the abilities of software applications that are currently found throughout our everyday life: *digital assistants face recognition, photo captioning, financial solutions, and product suggestions.*

The challenging part regarding integrating AI or ML into an application is not the technology, or the math, or the scientific research or the algorithms. The challenge is getting the version deployed into a production environment as well as maintaining it operational and sustainable. Software application advancement groups understand exactly how to deliver company applications as well as cloud services. AI/ML groups know exactly how to develop designs that can change a company. However, when it pertains to placing both with each other to implement an application pipeline certain to AI/ML-- to automate it and cover it around good implementation techniques-- the procedure needs some effort to be effective.

4. RPA & DEVOPS

Automate DevOps with RPA (Robotic Process Automation)

Lately among many DevOps expert proceeded and initiated the knowledge transition (KT) adhering to the practice.

While great info was recorded throughout the knowledge transition, it is always hard to take an entire dump of years of knowledge that a person holds. Even more it takes some time for people taking control of to learn the nuances at work.

With a seasonal skill shortage, sicknesses and also web traffic delays, we had to support the solution demands. Entering into individual's role and working towards resolving support tickets assists you comprehend the difficulties and also possibilities.

We try to be forward looking. At the very same time we count on the "*You educate a person to hunt* ..." ideology and for this reason train the juniors until they come to be independent, after that delegate and proceed to the next obstacle.

But after that the length of time could we keep doing this? There are a number of "mundane", "average" as well as "repeat" tasks that must be carried out with *Robot procedure automation.*

Suppose we needed to train a person who did not "proceed", "obtain stuck in web traffic" or "fall sick". So we have to launch a KT (knowledge transition) workout to educate a bot, quickly we would recognize the possibilities and also benefits.

Now a person would certainly suggest that there are choices to do automation using scripting, command line, API and so on. Possibly a lot more reliable! In reality DevOps groups do keep this pursuit of automating using these alternatives and increase their maturity. The obstacle is that scripting not only needs core technological skills yet likewise capacities revealed in the underlying layer of all the tools being used in business process flow to enable scripting.

For RPA, functional skills suffice. The benefit with RPA is that it is a *direct substitute of human actions utilizing the very same tool.* Thus individuals doing the functional jobs are encouraged with capacity to improve their performance through automation.

Robot procedure automation provides an excellent chance to improve DevOps maturity.

Robotic process automation: Why IT Ops requires leading

Robot process automation (RPA), a type of software that imitates the steps that human beings take when executing a task within a process, has been hailed as an important aspect for triggering digital improvement, as an inexpensive option to DevOps and active investments, and as an essential technology for minimizing costly, very hand-operated jobs across business.

However while most analysts concur that these robots

have legs-- forecasting *significant growth for the modern technology in the next 5 years*-- there have actually additionally been numerous failings. Right here's why IT need to solidify their assumptions for the innovation, as well as IT procedures ought to play a key role, involving with business to aid get deployment right.

Just how does RPA Affect IT as well as DevOps?

By encouraging organization customers, Robotic Process Automation augments advancement and IT resources for organization's growth. Especially, where minimal resources are stretched across a seemingly unlimited number of repetitive tasks.

Company decision-makers get tired of hearing *'what do you want me to put on hold'* when determining a brand-new development concern. Robot Process Automation (RPA) can include a device to the IT as well as a service toolkit to change that by permitting durable automation that requires much less IT resources and infra.

So, is RPA really empowering the DevOps team by using robust, governable innovation promising much faster and also cheaper production cost? While RPA can provide significant price savings and get rid of tiresome jobs for IT/DevOps workers, it can likewise show up as a difficult modern technology to regulate.

RPA - Disruptive technology at the office
Prior to we look specifically at the influence of RPA on DevOps teams, it may be valuable to give a quick review of just how RPA systems work and also why this newest turbulent innovation is brought in a lot of focus by midmarket companies.

Robot Process Automation *mimics human actions without*

modification to the existing, underlying modern technology framework. RPA is technology agnostic, code-free, and also can function across tradition ERPs, data processors, custom applications, and also any kind of various other kinds of IT systems. If it can be utilized by a human, it can be utilized by an RPA robot.

Due to the fact that RPA interacts with software through the existing application's user interface, no coding or assimilation is called for. This means, from an IT/DevOps viewpoint, their bit to change and also typically little to do. And, since there is no coding or assimilation, you can release an RPA solution in a matter of days or weeks-- rather than months or perhaps years. These two elements, the *lack of coding and also the rate of release,* aid Robotic Refine automation provide a rapid ROI and also ongoing cost financial savings-- which is why it's generating such a buzz.

A straight difficulty-- or a unique chance for DevOps groups?

Should IT/DevOps employees press back at RPA? Robotic Process Automation does have the prospective to replace lots of traditional development possibilities in the 'API Economy.' As soon as trained, the RPA software program adheres to the details process, immediately refines deals, adjusts data, activates feedbacks, as well as communicates with various other systems. A technology lowers the requirement for people to do high-volume IT support, process design, software application testing, remote infrastructure, and also back-office processes, which hare tasks discovered throughout midmarket enterprises. So yes, in this way, RPA does have the possibility to interfere with the IT landscape. Yet it's even more likely that RPA will certainly produce additional opportunities for modern technology workers.

Just as it assures cost-free company individuals from executing high-volume, low-value jobs, RPA can free IT personnel to handle much more essential, fascinating, and also challenging work. There is an around the world shortage of knowledgeable IT individuals, and the spreading of software program growth boot camps attests to this. *RPA can give the stimulate that moves individuals up the value chain, providing opportunities for greater worth and also greater reward employment.* Additionally, the advancement and also maintenance of RPA innovation will certainly itself supply brand-new task chances.

The Institute for Robotic Refine Automation agrees, as it noted in its RPA guide: *"Though it is expected that automation software application will certainly replace approximately 140 million full-time workers worldwide by the year 2025, many top quality tasks will certainly be created for those that have the ability to preserve and also boost RPA software program."*

Another means RPA can actually enhance employment possibility is through *reshoring*-- bringing previously contracted out tasks back under the company roofing system. Within the IT division, employees can assist in identifying new jobs ripe for automation, as well as establish brand-new, complementary applications and interfaces. By lowering, and even removing outsourcing, Robot Process Automation has the potential to advertise new work creation, and placed business securely in control of their tasks and also resources.

Face problems directly
As RPA proceeds to get approval amongst midmarket companies, concerns for possibility of *job losses* or the demand for new abilities are inescapable. Smart firms will intend to acknowledge as well as resolve these issues in order to get wide approval and make the transition to ever-more automated IT facilities.

In practically every sector of our economy, technology

interrupts well-known means of getting jobs done. Forward-thinking IT, as well as DevOps personnel, is smart, clever, and in much demand. Maybe much more swiftly as well as extra enthusiastically than any kind of another kind of worker, these folks will certainly discover how to take advantage of brand-new technologies as well as discover new methods to produce added worth for the business.

DevOps with RPA

With automation playing a vital function in DevOps, DevOps Integration with RPA (Robotic Process Automation) will create brand-new transformation in the Automation landscape and getting rid of human intervention to specify system driven DevOps pipe ex. CI/CD, Continuous Testing, and so on.

DevOps integration with RPA will arise as the key bars to develop the best-in-class organization. They have to reveal calculated management in sustaining their parent's RPA as well as DevOps Integration transformation as well as journeys. This integration will undoubtedly lead to calculated service transformation success for enterprise course. Digital transformation is the supreme objective for each business; this will be the essential criteria to achieve success.

In much less than a decade, the cloud technology in the business has gone from being the *exemption to the standard*. Stress to consumerism IT requires consumer-facing firms to progress their cloud capacities, reconsider how job obtains done, accept new techniques, and adapt to evolving customer preferences.

We'll have to look at the below factors for adoption:

- Current modern technology maturation levels across consumer-facing markets.

- Exactly how cloud, DevOps, Agile, and also robotic process automation (RPA) can multiply organization impacts when applied with each other.

- How Agile principles can change organization features and also allow venture agility, consisting of specific market usage cases.

Individuals will learn how leading companies are changing by relocating beyond the cloud and also broadening Agile as well as DevOps right into organization functions.

Sample RPA (Robotics Process Automation) DevOps Engineer- Job Post

Must have
- Knowledge of Robotic Process Automation (RPA) tools such as UiPath, Blue Prism, and also in certain Automation Anywhere Enterprise (AAE).

- The expertise of the Development of robotics making use of the RPA application, in certain AAE.
- Expertise in English that enables free conversations in a company environment.

Nice to have.
- Research & Development in the advancement and application of new RPA remedies.
- Administration as well as Life Process Administration with RPA-type applications.
- Experience in automation using scripting languages.
Exactly how we work.
At XXX, we comply with the agile method, utilizing

versatile structures like Scrum as well as Kanban at our daily job.

We are innovative, and we rely on people we collaborate with. The broad autonomy our staff members have promotes inspiration as well as creative thinking what allows us to adjust to the transforming demands of company companions.

Small systems called squads are the core of our organization. They have a clear vision of items, get rid of obstacles autonomously, and, based upon team teamwork, exercise one of the most adaptable as well as an efficient method of functioning.

Operate in a group with IT competences in the areas of Robotics Process Automation. I am performing R&D works as well as "life process management" for the aforementioned areas. Engagement in the transfer and launch of RPA solutions within the XXX group entities, generally in Europe (including international delegations).

Range of tasks

- Research & development RPA: 60%.
- Introducing as well as transferring RPA solutions: 20%.
- Business trips: 20%.

Various other needs

- Greater technical education and learning (or presently a student) favored the IT profile.
- Full freedom at the office, in the location of pointed out over innovations and also obligations at the workplace.
- Experience in executing as well as supervising RPA sort of application atmospheres, particularly AAE.
- Analytical believing in the location of understanding as

well as translating business and financial procedures.
- Understanding of Agile strategy as well as Scrum framework.
- Readiness to sometimes take place service trips.
- Accountable, stress-resistant, ability to make fast and accurate choices, dependable, communicative, imaginative.
- Ability to operate in a group.

Few Examples where AI& ML have contributed to DevOps:

With automation playing a vital function in DevOps, DevOps Integration with RPA (Robotic Process Automation) will create brand-new transformation in the Automation landscape and getting rid of human intervention to specify system driven DevOps pipe ex. CI/CD, Continuous Testing, and so on.

Basic Concepts: Cut the Clutter

The Refine of automating the workflows with the help of robots/software to lower the participation of human beings is claimed to be Robot Refine Automation.

Robot: Entities that simulate human activities are called Robotics.

Process: Sequence of actions that bring about a significant activity. For instance, the process of making tea or your preferred dish, etc

Automation: Any procedure which is done by a robotic without human treatment.

5. REAL STUFF
(CASE STUDIES/PRACTICAL EXAMPLES/COMPANIES)

So, yeah!! Enough of theory.

But that was necessary to get the hold of things and understand that how these emerging technologies are related with DevOps, advantages of their intertwining and limitations of applying them in DevOps culture.

As a Technology Consultant and someone who has to chalk out digital strategy for technologically laggard entities more often, we are asked simple questions like:

- Can you share real time implementation case studies where AI and ML worked alongside DevOps culture

- How were the results? Did they save any money?

- What are the security implications? Is my data safe if we use ML and AI in DevOps development methodology?

- After your team is done rolling out the applications, will our team would be able to manage it? What new skillets we have to acquire to manage an application developed using DevOps+ ML+AI?

- Who are the major players in this space, what are the latest products used?

So, let's see what are the latest news, trends and case studies which can give us relevant answers!

A) AIOPS

1. Epsilon Case Study -AIOPS Implementation

About Epsilon

Operational Since: 1969
Revenues: $2.2 billion
Employees: 8,000

Epsilon is a leading service provider of multichannel, data-driven modern technologies as well as advertising solutions. It provides marketing and company services, both online as well as offline, sustained by the wealthiest analytics, insights, and data in the industry. The agency takes care of different loyalty programs, custom-made data sources and SaaS marketing options on the part of its Lot of money 500 customers, acting like a. Managed advertising and marketing provider.

Issues Faced

Epsilon is an advertising and marketing solution and also a technology carrier to leading Lot of money 500 brands. The company's IT procedures team, Shared Technology Service (STS), is an enterprise-wide group

That sustains the business's income generation by giving a

platform-as-a-service support model for its different items and also services. The company has seven inner organization units as well as numerous clients. The interior company units, as well as clients, run a few of their own IT framework, run by their very own IT teams. Business devices, as well as clients, also make use of a common framework that is handled and kept by STS.IT framework assets and also solutions are distributed across datacenter (server, storage, network, virtualization, and container) and also multi-cloud (AWS, Azure workloads. STS made use of a mix of IT operations devices from different suppliers like CA Solution Desk for solution monitoring, Solar Winds for monitoring and Windows Web Server Update Provider (WSUS) for patching

Right here are a few of the operational maintenance and also oversight challenges encountered by the STS teams:

- With service units frequently spinning up and also retiring hybrid workloads, it was ending up being a burden to onboard, display, as well as keep hybrid IT possessions in line with customer and also corporate plans for administration, safety and also compliance.

- Despite all the investments in various tools, the firm battled to manage thousands of IT facilities assets and solutions across streamlined IT teams and dispersed business groups.

Solution

Epsilon executed AIOPS Solution as a scalable IT operations platform for uncovering, monitoring, patching, and automating a global infrastructure footprint of greater than 20,000 IT assets throughout seven internal company units and numerous clients. Right here's just how the firm gained visibility as well as control of its enormous IT footprint making use of AIOPS Solution:

The Solution

- *Asset Visibility.* With a multi-tenant platform developed for dispersed range, AIOPS Solution supplies presence of crossbreed work for its international service units. The STS group obtains a unified sight of all their infrastructure assets via AIOPS Solution's policy-based discovery that delivers automatic and quick on boarding of gadgets throughout worldwide locations.

- *Monitoring Automation.* With AIOPS Solution's monitoring plans, STS has the ability to drive keeping track of consistency and also customization for its entire infrastructure. IT groups can apply the very same monitoring template for a certain work across all their service units. At the very same time, the AIOPS Solution monitoring structure uses personalized monitoring in a. self-service, user-defined manner. Best of all, STS can swiftly understand if all IT assets are being kept track of properly without needing to deal with numerous siloed tools.

- *Patching Scale.* AIOPS Solution's spot monitoring plans provide a durable option for. Accelerating patch rollouts throughout its hybrid infrastructure. STS gains visibility for both Windows and Linux server patching in a solitary place and accomplishes systematized reporting for patch installment status and also failings. Most importantly, IT teams can arrange device teams by company unit, develop automated patch timetables for various devices, and also meet inner plans for conformity.

- *Automation.* AIOPS Solution's runbook automation framework (that improves asset. monitoring and also unified monitoring plans) helps STS drive towards the auto. Removal of crucial concerns without human treatment. Additionally, STS expects. basic operating procedures within runbooks to make it possible for agile occurrence response, faster mean time to fix, and also quicker recovery.

2. Carousel Case Study -AIOPS Implementation

About Carousel

Founding Year: 1992
Revenues: $550 million
Employees: 1,300
Customers: 6,000

Headquartered in Exeter, Rhode Island, Carousel Industries (Carousel) is an identified leader in helping organizations develop the way they interact and orchestrate the flow of info throughout their networks.

While the business was widely active with 6,000 clients and also working with most of the global Fortune 500, the company encountered operational challenges for scaling their Managed Services. Review just how Carousel developed a Business Command Facility and acquired real-time occurrence administration capacities for legacy and also modern workloads with AIOPS solution.

Issues Faced

Devices Overload. The business had separate management systems for Syslog monitoring, SNMP monitoring, patch management, network setup backups, and UC efficiency monitoring.

Manual Labor. There was no unified system that might efficiently automate workloads.

Functional Silos. With greater complexity and hybrid IT, case resolution needed more time, effort, as well as much more knowledgeable personnel.

Manual Asset Exploration and On boarding: he on boarding process would certainly take weeks or months as a result of missing out on auto-discovery for gadgets, network connectivity, as well as application traffic.

Solution

Enterprise Command Facility: A new solution delivery platform AIOPS solution for IT operations management and ServiceNow for IT service monitoring.

Devices Consolidation: Framework tracking manages the lifecycle of web server computing resources while AIOps consumes, analyzes, and also refines occasions from different network tracking devices.

Organizational Effectiveness: Carousel reduced the expense of solution delivery by accepting necessary operating procedures using runbook automation for scalable and effective service delivery.

Benefits

Decreased headaches from alert storms: Carousel's event management team can identify origin triage cases quicker with a 95% reduction in alert sound from the AIOps reasoning engine.

Cost savings on resources with device combination as well as labor force optimization: By minimizing toolsets and also removing repeated, regular tasks using automation, the Carousel team saw a 20% decrease in labor and operational prices.

Improved Web Marketer Rating: With faster, a lot more boosted service delivery, Carousel took pleasure in a 30% improvement in complete client satisfaction.

3. Green Pages Case Study -AIOPS Implementation

About Green Pages

Founding Year: 1992
Revenues: $130 million
Employees: 200

GreenPages is a leading systems integrator as well as cloud services company with yearly earnings of $130 million. GreenPages required an excellent IT operations monitoring platform that would certainly drive their following level of solution delivery. Read the study to learn how GreenPages has had the ability to sustain even more customers, come to be extra positive in its solution delivery, as well as origin out operational inadequacies.

Challenge: Provide world-class IT functional as well as management solutions at the range to customers

Solution: Offers managed IT services, including transformation services, cloud services, contemporary IT, and also conventional IT options.

With AIOPS Solution multi-tenant as well as cloud-based design, GreenPages was able to release swiftly and onboard customers in as little as a month.

According to Smith, "AIOPS Solution incorporates wide modern technology monitoring with application solution recognition as well as deep analytics. With AIOPS Solution, GreenPages can centralize every one of our functional activities and also give precisely the degree of service our clients require when they require it." AIOPS Solution. Assimilations for usual architectures, as well as innovations, are readily available out of the box saving. GreenPages hrs of custom development job. AIOPS Solution enables GreenPages to be truly federated by allowing its NOC, procedures, design, as well as.

Service delivery teams, customers, as well as even 3rd party vendors to view a single resource of fact. "This.

Enables us to provide exactly the level of solution our customers need when they require it," specifies Smith. AIOPS Solution facilities tracking, patching, troubleshooting, and administration reporting have been. Vital to taken care of solutions distribution at GreenPages. Different teams at GreenPages use AIOPS Solution to remain on top of vibrant hybrid IT settings:

The Remedy

- *Solution Distribution.* The NOC solutions group makes use of AIOPS Solution for alerting, occasion handling, and also the implementation of typical operating treatments.

- *Availability & Efficiency.* The operations groups leverage AIOPS Solution for troubleshooting. Complicated occasions and problems and also remote access to client atmospheres for problem remediation as well as alter management.

- *Coverage.* The service distribution team heavily leverages the coverage and also the administration capabilities within AIOPS Solution.

- *Pre-Sales.* Beyond managed services, the AIOPS Solution platform is used by engineer's and. application engineers to help with discovery as well as layout services.

Benefits: GreenPages NOC and even procedures teams can use a single administration system for all tasks. GreenPages has actually raised efficiencies and lowered intricacies as well as prices connected with using several toolsets.

4. NIIT Technologies Case Study -AIOPS Implementation

About NIIT Technologies

FOUNDING YEAR: 2004

REVENUES: $338 MILLION

TOTAL EMPLOYEES: 9000

NIIT Technologies is an international IT services company that provides top quality solutions to 250+ consumers across 18 countries. NIIT Technologies aids business in optimizing their facilities by reducing the intricacy of technology as well as procedures.

Challenge: Delayed troubleshooting of crucial cases. The same issues being reported via different devices.

Solution:

AIOPS Solution supplied several benefits that were important for managed services shipment at NIIT. With its cloud-based architecture, AIOPS Solution provided enterprise-grade safety, ease of fostering, as well as rapid provisioning.

"AIOPS Solution enables us to link IT procedures management and also straighten critical organization services with IT solutions for faster problem resolution. We can hurry sufficient to meet the requirements of our customers. AIOPS Solution's SaaS system helps NIIT Technologies combine occasions as well as alerts from application and infrastructure elements into a single framework.

NIIT's service shipment groups utilize AIOPS Solution to monitor cases happening across the customer settings in real time:

- *Functional Exposure.* AIOPS Solution supports diverse IT settings across traditional datacenters, public clouds, and also personal cloud framework. NIIT Technologies can manage cases, adjustments, as well as problems for crossbreed cloud settings without deploying multiple tools.

- *Combination Structure.* AIOPS Solution provides broad integrations that link the community of Enterprise IT administration devices. AIOPS Solution's assimilation framework enabled NIIT Technologies to reduce down the moment invested in triaging events by 80%.

- *Automation.* With AIOPS Solution, NIIT Technologies has decreased hands-on tasks by nearly 40%. The taken care of the solutions team can perform routine tasks on a regular timetable as well as. Respond to unanticipated activities via event-driven activities.

- *Audit Trails.* AIOPS Solution console recordings provide a trusted audit route for accessibility, login, and also task within a client's IT setting. Console recordings are a vital component of conformity and audit processes at NIIT Technologies.

Benefits: AIOPS Solution has enabled NIIT Technologies to retire several point tools for monitoring (servers, networks, storage, and databases) and service management (ticketing, patching, and incident management). With multiple tools having been phased out, NIIT Technologies has saved more than $100,000 in licensing costs in the first year alone.

AIOPS VENDORS								
Data Agnostic Tool	Anodot	Bigpanda	Evolen	Fixstream	Foglogic	Loom	Moogsoft	Opsramp
Legacy Platform	bmc	Ca	IBM	Microfocus				
Logging	Devo	elastic	OverOps	Scalyr	Splunk	Sumo Logic		
Monitoring	Appdynamics	NewRelic	Dynatrace	ScienceLogic	SignalFx	Virtual Instruments	OpsRamp	
Alerting	Pagerduty	OpsRamp						

B) MLOPS

While researching on MLOPS latest news we came across a conference held in Sep 2019 and that gave us access to the latest innovators in the field. So let's look at the companies working in this interesting space, solutions they offer and direction in which the industry is heading in 2020 and beyond.

Expert Opinions and data

"Getting machine learning into production is the No. 1 problem, that's why there are initiatives around MLOps. That's exactly what it is designed for."- **David Aronchick, Head of open source machine learning strategy, Microsoft**

"Core skills and job titles for your Operationalisation team will include source system experts, system architects, system administrators, application developers, and process engineers."- **Eric Brethenoux, VP and analyst, Gartner**

"One of the things we're trying to address with the project is there is a diversity of tools in our [use] cases and standards that we're working with within the machine learning ecosystem. We're trying to provide a way, with a solid platform, that allows people to leverage back best practices no matter if they're using TensorFlow or PyTorch."- **Thea Lamkin, open source program manager Google**

Only 47% of machine learning models are making it into production- **Gartner**

Major Players in MLOPS space

1. ParallelM & DataRobot

So, below is the latest news for the company

June 20, 2019

DataRobot and ParallelM — The Future of MLOps is Here

BY PARALLELM

ParallelM, the pioneer in MLOps, has become part of DataRobot, the leader in automated machine learning and a true innovator in AI.

At ParallelM, our mission is to help our customers realize the value of AI through technology to deploy, manage, and govern machine learning models from any machine learning platform or framework on any cloud or on-premise. As it turns out, DataRobot shares our mission of delivering value from AI, our culture of innovation, and sees the need for MLOps in the market.

The truth is that this is just the beginning of MLOps and Governance. Companies and analysts are just starting to understand the need for a system of record for machine learning models and applications being created across organizations and how to govern them. With the support of DataRobot, we know that we can get the MLOps message to more people and accelerate the development of an industry-leading MLOps product.

MLOPS product details:

MCenter: Deploy and Manage models in production

MCenter aids Information Scientists release, take care of, and also control ML versions in production. Just import your existing version from your favorite note pad, and after that, create information links or a REST endpoint for design offers with the drag-and-drop pipe home builder. Advanced keeping track of immediately creates informs when models are not running as anticipated because of altering data. With integrated design governance, every activity is controlled and also tracked, including model versioning, as well as who can promote versions into manufacturing to make sure compliance with policies.

Capabilities:

MCenter makes it very easy to release machine learning models with pre-built components and a pipeline builder to develop combinations of pipelines called MLApps.

Production Pipeline Builder-- MCenter features a collection of components and also a drag-and-drop pipeline builder so you can develop manufacturing pipelines in minutes, not hours.

Advanced ML Health Tracking-- MCenter automatically notifies you when production information departs from training data or when your model's outcomes begin to drift in addition to a canary model you trust so you can concentrate on building brand-new models and also only update models when required.

Integrated A/B Testing-- Verify that brand-new model are better than incumbents with built-in A/B screening with easy to review outcomes.

Complete Model Governance-- MCenter includes control and tracking for all actions taken in the system so you can regulate that can put models right into production as well as see what model supplied a provided forecast.

Building Advanced MLApps-- With MCenter, you can incorporate multiple pipelines together right into an ML application to serve your business usage case. Common pipeline mixes consist of automated batch re-training with REST reasoning, ensemble models, as well as consecutive pipelines where numerous pipelines feed each various other to develop a result

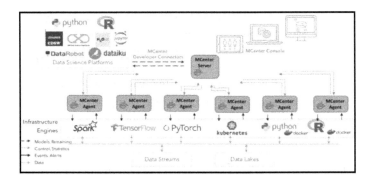

How it works: Diagram from parallelm.com

Agents-- Team triggers analytics engines and take care of local ML pipes. They give visibility right into the activity of the pipe and sends out notifies, occasions, and also stats to the server. They work with popular analytic engines including Spark, TensorFlow, as well as Flink

Server-- The server coordinates ML Applications as well as pipelines using the representatives. It implements policies, takes care of arrangement, and sends information to the console. The server enables automation of all the essential tasks connected to the release and administration of ML.

Versatile Deployment Options-- It can be deployed in the cloud, on-premise, or in hybrid scenarios. It also works throughout dispersed computing styles that consist of inter-operating, numerous analytic engines (Flicker, TensorFlow, Kubernetes, PyTorch, as well as a lot more). It functions with you to specify the most effective deployment setup for your details needs

Regarding DataRobot *(DataRobot acquired ParallelM)*

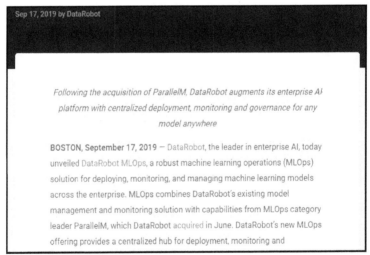

The company is the leader in enterprise AI and the category designer, as well as the leader in automated ML. Organizations worldwide use DataRobot to empower the teams they already have in place to swiftly develop and deploy machine learning models and also create sophisticated AI applications.

With a library of numerous one of the most powerful open source machine learning algorithms, the DataRobot platform encapsulates every finest technique and secure to accelerate and scale data scientific research abilities while optimizing openness, precision, and collaboration.

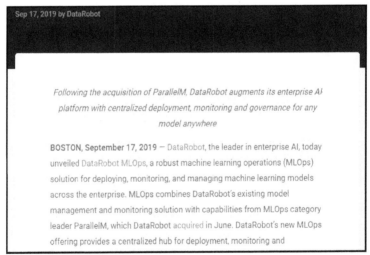

Sep 17, 2019 by DataRobot

Following the acquisition of ParallelM, DataRobot augments its enterprise AI platform with centralized deployment, monitoring and governance for any model anywhere

BOSTON, September 17, 2019 — DataRobot, the leader in enterprise AI, today unveiled DataRobot MLOps, a robust machine learning operations (MLOps) solution for deploying, monitoring, and managing machine learning models across the enterprise. MLOps combines DataRobot's existing model management and monitoring solution with capabilities from MLOps category leader ParallelM, which DataRobot acquired in June. DataRobot's new MLOps offering provides a centralized hub for deployment, monitoring and

Diagram from DataRobot website

The percentage of AI models produced but never took into production in large businesses has been approximated to be as much *as 90% or more*. With massive financial investments in information scientific research groups, systems, and framework, the number of AI projects is considerably rising-- in addition to the variety of missed opportunities. However, most projects are not revealing the value that company leaders expect and are presenting brand-new threats that need to be managed.

MLOPS Solution

MLOps solution provides the capacities that Information Science, as well as IT Ops groups, needs to function with each other to deploy, keep track of, as well as handle maker understanding models in manufacturing and also to control their use in production settings.

With MLOps as well as Governance, a business can:

- Quickly deploy artificial intelligence tasks from any type of ML system on contemporary production infrastructures such as Kubernetes and Spark on any type of cloud or on-premise.
- Screen ML-based applications for performance issues with ML-centric capabilities like data drift analysis, model-specific metrics, and infrastructure surveillance and alerts.
- Take care of the dynamic nature of artificial intelligence applications with the ability to frequently update designs, examination brand-new, competitive models, and also modification applications on-the-fly while continuing to offer service applications.
- Implement governance policies associated with ML deployment and also record the data that is needed for solid governance methods, including who is publishing versions, why modifications are

being made, as well as what models remained in the area over time.

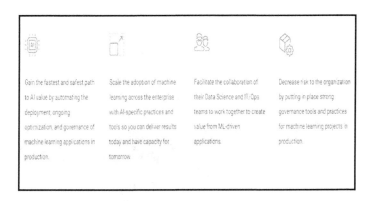

Gain the fastest and safest path to AI value by automating the deployment, ongoing optimization, and governance of machine learning applications in production.	Scale the adoption of machine learning across the enterprise with AI-specific practices and tools so you can deliver results today and have capacity for tomorrow.	Facilitate the collaboration of their Data Science and IT/Ops teams to work together to create value from ML-driven applications.	Decrease risk to the organization by putting in place strong governance tools and practices for machine learning projects in production.

Data Robot MLOPS Solution from their website

2. DataBricks

DataBricks automates numerous actions of the data scientific research process including increased data preparation, visualization, function engineering, hyperparameter tuning, model search, and ultimately automated version tracking, reproducibility, and deployment, via a combination of indigenous product offerings, partnerships, and also customized options for a fully controlled and clear AutoML experience. See as an example exactly how you can run hyperparameter adjusting at scale on DataBricks with improved Hyperopt as well as MLflow combination:

111

Diagram from DataBricks website

3. Iguazio

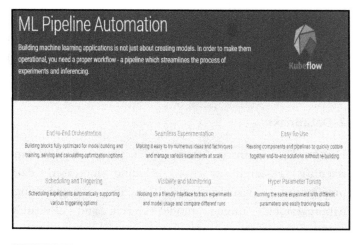

The research Platform gives a turnkey solution to establish and deploy machine learning models. It comes with vital integrated applications: artificial intelligence and also machine learning frameworks such as KubeFlow, Glow as well as TensorFlow along with orchestration tools like Docker as well as Kubernetes as well as a variety of bespoke server less features.

The system allows synchronized access through numerous industry-standard APIs for streams, tables, things, and also data that are all saved and also normalized once, to make sure that clients can introduce brand-new jobs and also after that take in, share and also examine data much faster.

By linking the space between development and procedures, business no more takes care of the complexity of relocating work with various pipes. Iguazio's end-to-end complete solution enables users to run training and production models in one platform, all closer to the information source.

In the training stage, data scientists run questions on huge datasets to create algorithmic models and also firmly share them with licensed users. When it's time to place these models right into production, Iguazio makes it possible for real-time processing of streaming data for quick time to understandings. Considering that machine learning models are integrated into containers, they are easily relocated from growth settings to operational environments. The Iguazio system supplies unequaled fine-grained safety where information gains access to or auditing can be imposed, utilizing the multi-layered network, identification, metadata, or content-based policies.

4. Metis Machine now Skafos

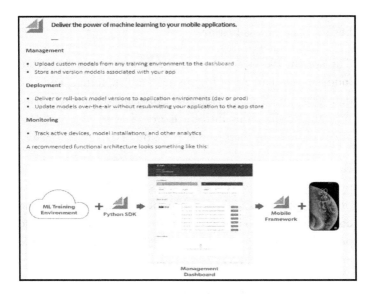

Machine Learning for your Mobile Apps

- Quickstart ML Tasks
- Bring Your Own Models
- Seamless Deployments
- ML Model Versioning
- Monitoring & Analytics
- Infrastructure Agnostic
- Framework Agnostic
- Model Delivery   Validation

5. Hydrosphere.io

A Case – hydrosphere.io solutions for AdTech company, results delivered:

- Machine Learning operations got **scaled** from **2** models to **200+** models in production

- Stabilised and solidified Machine Learning pipelines gave **$20M of annual savings**

- ML Team productivity doubled, estimated **ROI increase** is $1M per year.

- Data science production iterations went seamless saving minimum 2 weeks of **time per release>**

- The demand for DevOps people presence in release chain was eliminated completely delivering a solid **improvement** to ownership **costs** and ROI.

- A month of **man-hours** for product management and a 3 months for QA are **saved** per release.

- Apache Spark jobs **completion rate** reached **99%**

- **Cluster throughput** increased 10 times saving $100K monthly.

- Facilitating over 10 products, implementation of the hyrosphere.io platform into AI/ML operations created a new **revenue stream** of $10M annually.

Diagram from Hydroshere.io website

6. Seldon

Solutions
Setting the new standard for ML ops

Designed to fit the way you work	**Data scientists**	**DevOps**	**Managers**
	Seldon liberates data scientists by reducing the amount of tasks that require support from DevOps teams and the time to operationalize models. This enables your data scientists to focus on building better models, to iterate faster and optimize based on real-world KPIs	DevOps teams hold the keys to production and are responsible for maintaining a scalable and secure infrastructure. Seldon gives your teams new machine learning superpowers based on rock-solid, cloud-native technologies, so they can focus on supporting production workflows and iterate at the pace that modern data science teams require to succeed.	Machine learning is the ultimate opportunity to revolutionise business. Managers are under increasing pressure to identify high value use cases, and move rapidly to production where KPIs can be evaluated and improved. Seldon empowers you by providing clearer insights and streamlining workflows between your data science and devops team.

Diagram from Seldon website

7. Datatron

Many teams discover that there's even more to simply releasing versions, which is currently a very hands-on as well as lengthy task. Datatron uses solitary version administration as well as administration platform for every one of your ML, AI, as well as Data Scientific research designs in production. We aid you automate, enhance, and accelerate your ML models to guarantee they are running smoothly and efficiently in production.

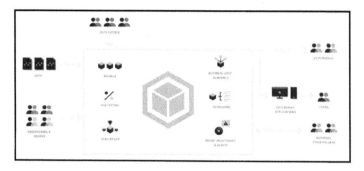

Diagram from Datatron website

ML Case Studies

1. Regeneron

Regeneron is a leading biotechnology company utilizing the power of scientific research to bring new medicines to clients in requirement

Challenges

Even more than 95% of all experimental medications that are currently in the drug growth pipe are anticipated to fall short.

To enhance these efforts, the Regeneron Genes Center developed one of the most detailed genetics databases by coupling the sequenced exomes as well as digital health and wellness documents of even more than 400,000 people. Nevertheless, they encountered countless challenges analyzing this enormous collection of data:

- Genomic as well as scientific data is very decentralized, making it extremely hard to evaluate as well as educate designs against their whole 10TB dataset

- Difficult as well as costly to scale their heritage architecture to sustain analytics on over 80 billion information factors

- Information teams were spending days just attempting to ETL the information so that it can be made use of for analytics

ML Solution

- *Automated cluster management*: streamlines the provisioning of collections, reducing the time invested in DevOps job so designers and information scientists can spend even more time overvalued tasks

- *Interactive workspaces*: permits data researchers to share information as well as understandings, promoting an atmosphere of openness as well as collaboration across the whole medication advancement lifecycle

- *Performance Spark-powered Pipes*: considerably improved integrity and speed of ETL pipelines made use of to process their 10TBs of EHR + DNAseq information

2. Sevatec

Sevatec is a high-technology solutions firm that leverages on technology innovation to overcome one of the most pressing challenges.

Challenges

- Tough to consume and also prepare data across 30+ diverse systems
- Assistance 2000+ customers who are siloed and also have the various capabilities (BI customers, statisticians, information designers, information scientists, company).
- Not have the capability to prepare a solitary view into the information for data science.
- Failure to scale their data science research initiatives as they were using RStudio on a single node.
- Utilized a range of disjointed tools to perform large information removals, which developed substantial DevOps intricacy.
- The system was being greatly taxed by really IO intensive questions, impacting their capacity to satisfy SLAs and also the needs of the remainder of their customer community.

ML Solution

ML solution has considerably simplified data design through a fully-managed cloud system as well as has increased data science by building a culture of collaboration and openness.

- Equalize access to data across their numerous data

118

- Resources via APIs and also data resource ports.
- Minimized access, a consume time from hrs to mins.
- Able to build machine learning models at range against the entire data collection
- Simplified framework management and also got rid of unnecessary DevOps work via automated and also protected collection monitoring
- Interactive work area allows numerous users to collaborate on the data and run data scientific research experiments that lead to cutting-edge machine learning designs

So, here we are:

1. This book is my attempt to update you on the unfolding story of AIOPS and MLOPS as "story to date. " I would certainly come out with the second part after a year as I am sure many new developments will unfold by the end of next year.

2. Beyond the apparent hustle and bustle of buzzwords and nomenclature every year, I genuinely believe that AI would drastically change the software development and deployment model in the next two years, and all these new startups would drive this change. It's astonishing how fast this cycle is moving. Especially for us who had seen the world before the internet came into our daily lives!!

Cheers to Continuous Growth!

Stephen Fleming

In case of any suggestions or queries, kindly reach out at:

Email: Valueadd2life@gmail.com
Facebook: @sflemingauthor

References

https://www.forbes.com/sites/janakirammsv/2018/11/04/the-growing-significance-of-devops-for-data-science/#f92f29c74817

https://www.veritis.com/blog/ai-powered-ml-driven-the-new-devops-trend/

https://techbeacon.com/enterprise-it/how-containerization-brings-ai-your-devops-pipeline

https://www.re-work.co/blog/why-use-machine-learning-in-devops

https://8allocate.com/article/how-to-optimize-devops-with-machine-learning/

http://www.ideas2it.com/blogs/ai-in-devops/

https://www.infostretch.com/ai-powered-predictive-bots-astute/

https://www.targetprocess.com/blog/artificial-intelligence-devops-automation/#The_Future_of_AI_and_DevOps_Automation

https://www.zdnet.com/article/ai-powered-devops-is-how-ca-wants-to-reinvent-software-development-and-itself/

https://www.mindtree.com/blog/cloud-devops-artificial-intelligence-new-troika-intelligent-it-infrastructure

https://gigaom.com/2019/01/11/hybrid-cloud-iot-blockchain-ai-ml-containers-and-devops-oh-my/

https://www.datasciencecentral.com/profiles/blogs/devops-for-machine-learning-ml-ai

https://dzone.com/articles/what-is-aiops-the-next-level-of-devops-services

https://azure.microsoft.com/en-us/blog/getting-ai-ml-and-devops-working-better-together/

https://devops.com/6-ways-ai-and-ml-will-change-devops-for-the-better/

https://www.kdnuggets.com/2018/02/applying-machine-learning-devops.html

https://content.intland.com/blog/using-artificial-intelligence-to-boost-agile/devops-efficiency

https://insidebigdata.com/2018/04/30/next-generation-devops-ml-ops/

https://www.agilestacks.com/products/machine-learning

https://www.infoq.com/articles/machine-learning-learn-devops

https://www.bterrell.com/robotic-process-automation-rpa/devops-on-their-heels

https://medium.com/@vsumedh/automate-devops-with-rpa-robotic-process-automation-25c617c73311

https://techbeacon.com/enterprise-it/robotic-process-automation-why-it-ops-needs-lead

https://devops.com/intelligent-devops-digital-systems/

https://www.linkedin.com/pulse/devops-rpa-manoj-jain/

https://www2.deloitte.com/us/en/pages/dbriefs-webcasts/events/january/2019/dbriefs-cloud-devops-rpa-and-enterprise-agility-bringing-it-all-together.html

https://www.ing.jobs/Global-NL/Vacature-details/RPA-Robotics-Process-Automation-DevOps-Engineer.htm

https://forum.uipath.com/t/rpa-infrastructure-promotion-between-environments-devops/69601

https://www.slideshare.net/SarahAnley/5-ways-to-use-itil-and-devops-for-rpa-operational-success

https://towardsdatascience.com/applying-machine-learning-to-devops-5fb7d69ac366

- Check out my last release!

The DevOps Engineer's Career Guide

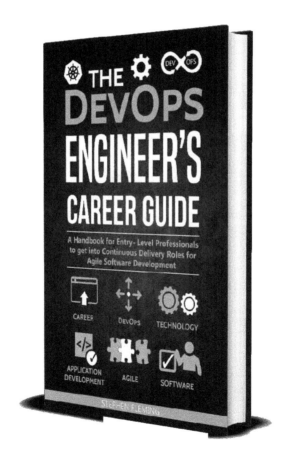

"Get Instant Access to Free Booklet and Future Updates"

- Link: http://eepurl.com/dge23r

OR

- QR Code: You can download a QR code reader app on your mobile and open the link: